# PUNCH!

## Why Women Participate in Violent Sports

Jennifer Lawler, Ph.D.

Wish Publishing
Terre Haute, Indiana
www.wishpublishing.com

LCCN: 2001093468

Proofread by Heather Lowhorn
Cover designed by Phil Velikan
Cover photo by arrangment with Corbis images

Printed in the United States of America
10 9 8 7 6 5 4 3 2 1

Published in the United States by
Wish Publishing
P.O. Box 10337
Terre Haute, IN 47801, USA
www.wishpublishing.com

Distributed in the United States by
Cardinal Publishers Group
7301 Georgetown Road, Suite 118
Indianapolis, Indiana 46268
www.cardinalpub.com

*For my daughter Jessica,*
*standing outside my office door, wanting to play:*
*here I come.*

# Table of Contents

# Acknowledgements

I must express my gratitude to my sister, Kathryn Lawler, for zealously hunting down every friend and acquaintance she could find who plays a contact sport or might know someone who does. Also, many thanks to Amy Bunker for putting me in touch with dozens of women who play contact sports. Without you two, I would still be trying to find people to interview for this book.

Special appreciation to everyone who took the time to talk with me about their experiences participating in or coaching contact sports. Without you, this book would never have been written.

# Preface

The idea for *PUNCH! Why Women Participate in Violent Sports* came to me when my mother asked, for the ninth time, why I played such a violent sport (Tae Kwon Do), in which I risked injury, in which I could hurt other people. Usually I dismissed her comments as the result of an over-protective mothering instinct, but this time I wondered if I were really all that different from other women—from women who don't play violent sports. I wondered what this meant about me and why I was, as an adult, so attracted to kicking and punching people when I had never been athletic in the past.

As an academic feminist, I was aware that the majority of feminists would not approve of my enjoyment of aggression. While I grieved over my excommunication from cultural feminism—the idea that men and women are naturally different and that women must somehow remain morally pure, nonviolent, and uncorrupted by a male-dominated society—I felt in my heart that I was a truer feminist than many of the scholars who disapproved of me and of women like me, because I knew something they did not: I knew that women had masculine traits that they could embrace instead of scorn. I knew that by finding and examining these traits and accepting them as part of who I was, I could be a fuller, more complete *person*—not a woman-victim, not a man-wannabe.

I felt sorry for the feminists who would never know what it was like to curl your fingers into a fist and execute a perfect punch. They would never know what it was to be strong and to know you were strong, to acknowledge that you had aggressive instincts, that you had anger, that you had power, and that you could channel all of these things in acceptable ways, in ways that did not hurt other people, or at least did not hurt other people who did not know what they were getting into.

I began considering my particpation in the martial arts— what it meant to me as a scholar and as a feminist, and why my mother was anxious about it, and why she seemed unable to accept my participation. I later realized that I was committing the sin of gender transgression, and she would have felt the same had my brother confided in her that he liked to wear ladies' undies. Not that he did. But if he had, her feelings would have been the same.

I found that I was not alone. I spoke with many women who also participated in contact sports and learned that they had heard similar concerns and objections from their families and friends, but that these concerns and objections had never stopped them from participating.

I began to wonder why. What was it about hitting other people that I found so appealing, that I would do it in spite of the disapproval of people I liked and respected? And, more universally, why did all of these other women find contact sports so appealing, that they would continue to play regardless of what the people around them thought—including some of their own teammates?

Thus the concept of the book was born—I would, as an observer-participant, using my own experiences to guide me, investigate research on women in sports, examine gender studies, and interview athletes and coaches to see if I could determine some areas of commonality among the women who participate in contact sports, few of whom see any relationship between what they do and any of the schools of feminist thought. Yet what they do could radically change what we believe women capable of, what we believe women should be and can do.

I did not—and do not—intend the book to be a definitive investigation of the causes and effects of women in contact sports, nor the last word on what critics say about women who participate in violent sports. Instead, I view the book as a preliminary conversation, a starting place from which we (as a community of interested participants and observers) might further elucidate the issues involved. As far as my own research has been able to turn up, *PUNCH! Why Women Participate in Violent Sports* is the first full-fledged examination of the reasons why women become involved—and stay involved—in contact sports.

The book does not posit a specific psychoanalytic viewpoint, nor does it position itself from a specific feminist perspective. It is not the work of a sociologist. My training is as a feminist literary critic. I think of this book as something akin to what a folklorist would do. What are women saying about their experiences in contact sports? What motifs and themes are common in these stories? What do the stories tell us about women—and about sports? When outsiders—sportswriters, other athletes, scholars, family members—criticize women who participate in violent sports, what does this say about them, the outsiders and the women both? What does it reveal about a culture's perceptions of women and their "feminine" attributes (or lack thereof)?

This does not mean that I ignored research conducted by

psychologists, sociologists, ethnographers and the like. I do incorporate research from a wide variety of fields, disciplines and theoretical approaches. However, I feel my purpose with this book is similar to what an investigative journalist does—here are the theories, here's what they say about women, here's how the women in question respond. I do not necessarily argue that one approach is superior to another, although I am admittedly biased in my belief that contact sports are—can be—good for women.

Lately, there has been considerable interest in how men and women differ from each other. Do they have genetic differences, or are their differences, even in terms of physical strength, a result of cultural expectations? Colette Dowling's book, *The Frailty Myth: Women Approaching Physical Equality*, strikes a resonant chord in me. From my experience in the martial arts, women are not, as a group, weaker than men. Some individual women are weaker than some individual men (and vice versa), which is not to say that they couldn't be stronger if they had started younger or believed they could be or lifted weights. However, this perspective/experience is not shared by all women in contact sports. Some of them say, flat out: "Women are weaker than men; the reason I participate in this sport is to make me as strong as possible." (Cox) Do I think women who express ideas such as these are wrong? No. I think their experiences might be different from mine.

I intend this book to be a bridge between two disparate groups of people: women in contact sports, who tend not to be interested in feminist theory and who do not necessarily connect their participation in a contact sport to any larger issues about women; and feminist scholars and other "outsiders" who have little understanding of contact sports and whose immediate reaction to it is that it must be bad and damaging for women.

This book is my contribution to a better understanding of why some women make some of the choices they do and what those choices mean to society at large.

— *Jennifer Lawler*
Lawrence, Kansas
*March 5, 2001*

# Introduction:
# Women and Violent Sports

When I was 27 years old, I hit a man hard enough to break his ribs. I did a lot of soul-searching afterwards.

I decided I liked it.

Like most women my age—like most women, period—I was trained to be a nice girl growing up. I spent most of my life following the litany of things nice girls do—and the things nice girls don't do. When you are raised to be a nice girl, the list of things you cannot do is long. But it's best if you memorize it. You wouldn't want to be mistaken for someone who's not nice.

You must always defer to other people, especially men. You must never swear in public. Or in private, either. You must always be polite and you must never say what you think. When you are a nice girl, you put your desires last. This is because you're nice and you want other people to know it (otherwise, what's the point?) You must always worry about the other person. You must ask yourself, what does that other person think? You must make sure you ask this question every time you encounter another person, which means you ask this question a lot.

Nice girls don't sweat in public. A nice glow, that's what they're allowed. They never raise their voices and they don't draw attention to themselves. Women who do—they're not our kind. They're not our class.

Nice girls do not hit men hard enough to break their ribs.

Sometimes I embarrass my mother, who only wanted me to grow up to be a nice girl, liked by other nice girls. She wanted me to marry a nice boy and live in the nice suburbs and procreate nice children.

Instead I married the first man who kicked me in the head.

I am a martial artist, as is my former husband. Neither of us is very nice. We have a daughter who is sweet and adorable, but we're hoping she doesn't turn out nice. I, for one, am hoping she learns how to break a man's ribs. It's a handy skill to have in a society that still violently suppresses women. Already I am teaching her how to perform a front kick, which she finds is handy for kicking a soccer ball around. If she wants to play soccer, that will be OK, too.

Vicky Anderson, a friend of mine, a black belt in Tae Kwon Do, has a daughter named Chantal who earned her black belt in Tae Kwon Do when she was twelve. Vicky says she never worried much about teenage boys getting out of hand with Chantal. She was never very afraid for her. Felt Chantal could protect herself. Felt Chantal could take care of herself.

That must be a nice feeling. It's not one my mother ever had. Most of us have mothers who want to protect us. Most of us have mothers who want to keep us safe from harm. To do so, they think we need to be nice girls so that people won't feel violently inclined toward us. So that we can attract the right kind of boys, the right kind of men. So that those men can protect us, keep us safe. Our mothers breathe sighs of relief when we finally get married. Now, they think, now she's safe. They know, if they really think about it, that we are no safer than before, but it's a nice illusion. It's the best a mother can do. Our mothers want us to be safe and free from harm.

That's why they can never understand us when we suddenly announce that we're participating in violent sports, that we are, essentially, seeking harm, that we're learning how to be martial artists or boxers or football players. They don't quite get why we would want someone to hurt us, someone to hit us, someone to train us how to hurt other people, how to hit other people. This is not something nice girls do.

Nice girls don't play violent sports. Even now, when women are encouraged to participate in sports, they are usually encouraged to play genteel sports such as tennis and swimming. The kinds of things you can do in the suburbs; that's what they have country clubs for. Or women are encouraged to play "womanly" sports, the kind of sports where you look pretty while you're playing, like gymnastics or diving. Although once you become a woman, these sports no longer really want you. If pressed, basketball will be allowed, soccer is acceptable. You use up a lot of energy playing these games; they're easy to understand: she shoots, she scores. And they're team sports, all the coaches and business executives say that team sports are good for you. Besides, there needs to be a place for all those tall girls, all those big girls who don't quite fit the standards for gymnastics or ballet. What better place than basketball and soccer? But football? Ice hockey? Boxing? Who are we kidding?

When I began taking Tae Kwon Do lessons, I was a nice girl. Polite. Well-mannered. Never raised my voice, never broke a sweat, never uttered a swear word in the hearing of other people, although occasionally my apartment echoed with the sounds of my suppressed rage.

I was in my mid-twenties, in graduate school, a little overweight, feeling a little isolated, when I drove by the strip mall on the other side of town from where I lived. In a tiny storefront, a couple had started a martial arts school. I had always been aware that the place existed, but I had never really thought it had anything to do with me. At least not until I quit smoking and gained weight and realized I was going to have to do something about my health and fitness. I wasn't going to die of cancer, since I had quit smoking, but if I didn't do something soon, I was going to die of a heart attack from being so fat and out of shape.

On that day, I stopped by the strip mall on an entirely different errand. The glass door that led to New Horizons Black Belt Academy of Tae Kwon Do had a plastic sign that said "Open." One of the owners was in, but no class was in session. Wide glass windows revealed an empty room about the size of the living room at my place, with tattered carpet from all those feet pivoting for all those kicks for all those years. A small vestibule with chairs and a tiny walled-off office had been carved into the back end of the space.

What can I say? I was alone and out of shape, a graduate student without very many friends. I needed a change. And the glorious thing about this little training hall in this little strip center was that it wasn't aerobics. Everyone kept telling me I needed to take aerobics in order to get into shape, but I just couldn't see it. What would be the point? Hopping around with a bunch of body-obsessed 18-year olds? I didn't like 18-year olds when I was 18. Why would I want to hang around them now? I had seen aerobics classes on television and when I walked past a nearby gym. I always shook my head, wondering, has there every been anything so ridiculous in the history of sports as the development of the aerobics class? It was, shall we say, unappealing to me. When I talk to other women in contact sports, they always chortle and laugh: "What was I going to do, take up water aerobics?" I have always understood their point perfectly.

I remember staring at the sign. "New Horizons" seemed kind of a nice name for a martial arts school. Wasn't that what I was looking for? Something new, a way of opening up the narrow little world I inhabited? I remember thinking that Tae Kwon Do was a form of karate, and that when I was a little girl, I had wanted to learn karate. Kung-fu, we called it, my brother and I, and we would let out blood curdling screams and attack each other with flattened hands. "Hi-yah!" we would shout. Or we would stalk each other with exaggerated high steps, like we saw Bruce Carradine perform on reruns in the afternoon before our mother turned off the television. We weren't allowed to watch shows like that.

When I was 9 or 10, I casually mentioned to my mother that I would like to learn karate. My mother, a pained expression on her face, pretended she had not heard what I said. This was her common response whenever I said things she did not want to hear, things that were painful to her: she pretended she could not hear me.

I learned how to yell in Tae Kwon Do. It is called a kihop, it comes from the solar plexus, where your chi (ki) is said to reside. When I kihop, you cannot help but notice. You cannot pretend you don't hear me.

At the time, I was single, and I could do as I liked with the money I made from teaching two classes a semester. I could spend it on food, or I could spend it on martial arts classes. I lived alone in a town some miles away from my family, who would surely disapprove (that was also part of the attraction). No one would have to know about this adventure, nobody but me. If I chose to tell someone, that was my own decision. But no one had to know. I could succeed, or I could fail miserably, and it wouldn't make any difference. It would have no bearing on whether my Ph.D committee agreed that I had passed my comprehensive examinations or not; it wouldn't have any significant impact on whether the guy who sat next to me in English 850: The Non-Chaucerian Poets would ever get around to asking me out.

There was something faintly sinister about learning a martial art. That was it. That did me in. That was the sum total, the entire reason I thought of learning Tae Kwon Do. I did not know one single solitary person who practiced martial arts. It would be nothing like aerobics, I imagined. There wouldn't be a lot of 18-year olds bouncing around in spandex unitards. I would learn mysterious and secret techniques, and I could use them on the bad men who haunted my dreams. I lived alone; I had been told what happened to women who lived alone, and I believed the tales.

I walked in. The owner, a petite blonde who could break four concrete blocks with a single punch, smiled when she saw me. I didn't know about the concrete blocks then, but she looked at me with such calm and confidence that I knew immediately I wanted some of that, whatever it was. I asked her, "Do you teach Tae Kwon Do here?" as if the sign out front weren't proof enough. She nodded and I said, "I would like to sign up."

That was how much I thought about it, how carefully I researched the possibilities; it was just pure luck that I had found the right place on the first try. But I didn't know how lucky I was until years later when I would meet other instructors at other schools and discover that not all martial arts instructors care about creating excellent, well-rounded martial artists. It is very important that when girls and women are introduced to contact sports, they are taught the skills they need to defend themselves. They should never be fair game for superior athletes until they have developed their own skills to an appropriate level. This principle escapes many coaches and sports organizers. But I did not know that at the time. I did not understand about selecting a well-regarded training program and a good coach. All I knew was that I wanted to learn the magic tricks that would keep me safe from harm.

When I started Tae Kwon Do, I was just on the verge of understanding that I had been sold a bill of goods all my life, that what I had thought was the natural order of things was a socially constructed fabrication. I was just learning that I was a feminist, and that women are still paid less than men for the same jobs. I was just learning that my mother was wrong when she said that strenuous exercise was dangerous for women. She was just repeating what she had been taught. Who was she to disbelieve?

Women and warrior spirit is not a combination that has inspired many poets. But it does inspire a lot of women. When I first began training in the martial arts, what attracted me to the training hall was the toughness I associated with it. It took a lot of discipline, I thought, to perform the techniques, which I knew in a vague way were unusual, even spectacular. I knew you had to be strong. That was what I wanted to be: strong. No one had ever thought of me like that, not my friends, not my family members. I was never the smart one either, but here I was in graduate school, working on my Ph.D., which none of the smart ones in the family had managed to do. It occurred to me that perhaps it wasn't preordained, that perhaps if I hadn't been strong previously it didn't mean I could never be strong.

Anyone who knew me 10 years ago would never have believed that I would go on to earn a black belt in a martial art. I am the last person anyone expected to do this. The last person. Anyone else but me. Because I wasn't athletic, because I avoided physical exertion with a vengeance, because I was a pacifist. I hated to watch boxing on television; I hated to watch football. It seemed nonsensical to me, all these people beating each other up for the entertainment of a crowd of low-brow ruffians. Cultured people, a group of which I gladly counted myself a member, did not go in for sideshow exhibitions like that, did not marvel at drawing blood.

But I had a great deal of unexpressed anger. I knew it was there, I simply tried never to do anything with it. It had seemed that people had always decided for me how my life was going to be, with the weight of their expectations and their plans. If I ever wanted to be something that did not fit into their image, and I did, I never said it out loud for anyone to ridicule. When I said I was going to graduate school, my family laughed at me. You see, I was never the smart one. I was the funny one, that's why they laughed at me, I was the clown, that was my purpose: to be laughed at.

If no one took me seriously, it was perhaps partly because I never took myself seriously. I could never be counted on to finish a thing, to carry it through to completion. But really, how much opportunity do you have when you are young? You go to high school, to college, you graduate, you are unexceptional: you are young, that is why you are unexceptional.

But the lack of respect I noted among my family and friends I took as a more tragic thing than simply a reflection of my youth. It made me angry all the time, it made me unpleasant, it made me frustrated. I can do things, I wanted to say, I can do things, there are things that I'm good at, things I can do that you can't. I did not know what these things were, but I set out to find them.

This is the small-minded quest of a child who grew up in a large family. You are never special, never unique, nothing you have ever done is unopposed. Someone else always did it first, and better than you.

When I broke my first board in Tae Kwon Do using a side-kick, my sister said, "Oh, I learned to break a board with my hand at a retreat one day." Perhaps she was sharing, perhaps she wanted to find a connection with me, but all I knew was that she was stealing my thunder again.

But amazingly, although competition was a byword in my family, it didn't matter after the first tension of frustration I felt. I knew better. I didn't care how many boards she broke with the palm of her hand, she wasn't training. She wasn't a martial artist. She wasn't as tough as I was. If she thought breaking a board with her hand during a retreat sponsored by the corporation she worked for had any meaning, that was fine. I knew better. I knew that a skill you acquire after 15 minutes of work is nothing to be proud of. I knew real skills required work and dedication and perseverance, that they required sweat and tears, and yes, at least a small amount of blood. I knew that to be tough, to have accomplished something worthwhile, took time, took focus. And I also knew that if she never understood this, it did not matter. It did not detract from me. Because after I started practicing martial arts, I no longer had to answer to anyone but me.

When I earned my black belt in Tae Kwon Do, only a small coterie of friends, people who had also earned their black belts, understood what it meant. Only a few people understood the satisfying crack the boards made when I broke them all at once, with one kick, on the first try. Outsiders could catch at the meaning a little, but they would never understand. They would never really get it until and unless they earned a black belt, too. Otherwise, they were among the uninitiated. They would never know if they were tough enough.

When I started taking lessons in the martial arts, I had been living on my own—alone—for some years. And during all that time, I heard a lot of advice, read a lot of articles about how to remain safe in a dangerous world. It became clear that while the world was dangerous for single women, single women were also dangerous for the world, but I wasn't quite able to articulate this thought at the time. All I knew was The List, the things you had to do to keep safe. If you didn't follow The List, and something bad happened, then you were responsible for it. And even if you did follow The List and something bad happened, your friends and family would scour your story trying to piece together what you might have done wrong, where you might have deviated from The List, so that they could blame you for what went wrong. Because if you followed The List and something bad happened anyway, why then it meant that something bad could happen to anyone, and The List was useless, it didn't work, it couldn't keep the fear at bay. Because that is what The List is about: living in fear.

The List goes something like this: keep your door locked and bolted. Ask for identification when someone comes to the door. Have a male voice on your answering machine. Get a guard dog. Get an unlisted number. Don't go out at night. Don't go out alone.

I followed The List for years. And then one day, I thought, why are people terrorizing me for trying to live a life? Why don't men have to follow The List? Are men not victims of crimes? Can't their homes be robbed, too? And then I realized that as a culture we do a great job of instilling fear into women and we pretend that if we live constricted, immobile lives, the fear will never become a reality.

I clearly remember reading an article by a police officer who said when threatened, a woman should do exactly what an attacker said. If she did so, she would be less likely to get hurt. At the time, I thought there might have been some facts to back him up, but I later learned there weren't. What, then, made people like this give out such damaging advice? Why counsel women to submit when there was no concrete evidence that submitting was less dangerous than resisting? Was it because the world out there, society at large, was in collusion? That the world out there wanted us to submit, to just get it over with, to not resist anything we were told to do?

It occurred to me that in all the information I had read about how women should try to stay safe from harm, it never occurred to anyone, not one single writer, that a woman could resist, that she could fight back, and *she might actually win*. It seemed as if it were always a given that a woman might fight back, but she was doomed to lose. Because all men are taller, stronger, more capable than all women?

I had had enough. No, I finally said. I can break a man's ribs with one punch. You can't scare me anymore.

It was a nice feeling to finally stop being scared all the time, *all the time.*

For a long time after I earned my black belt, I would assess every man I met in the same way: I can take him. Him, maybe not. I can take *him*. All my life people had been warning me that men were my opponents—as well as my heroes—until one day I realized that I was my own hero, and that men were just men. Some were inclined to crime and some weren't. And while I couldn't guarantee myself or anyone else that my black belt in Tae Kwon Do would keep me safe from all harm, I could rest assured that anyone who attacked me, even if they did manage to rape or murder me, or whatever their intention, I could rest assured that my attacker would wish he had chosen another target. That's all I ever wanted, a fighting chance. I was almost thirty before I got it.

We've come a long way since the third century B.C., when women who tried to participate in the Olympics would be summarily executed. In more recent times, they haven't been executed, but they've been excluded. Of course, that doesn't mean women didn't participate in sports in the past, they just didn't get much ink. And they had to withstand a lot of discouragement to play the games they wanted to play.

The history of women in sports has been one of ups and downs. Boxing between women was popular in Europe in the eighteenth century . . . but often the participants were topless and the point of the exercise was to titillate male viewers. The first American women's boxing match took place in 1876 and it was a respectable bout between fully clothed fighters. One woman, Nell Saunders, even became famous for her prowess in the ring. But by the early twentieth century, women's involvement in boxing was primarily as round card girls, those beauties who wear skimpy bathing suits and high heels and manage the difficult task of displaying a card listing the round number between one round and the next. The point couldn't be clearer: men are active participants in life; women are there to be looked at. If women aren't worth looking at, if they don't enjoy being ogled, they aren't worth much.

A number of studies and histories written about the participation of women in sports reveal the depth of women's involvement in sport, even during periods (such as the Victorian era) when they were routinely discouraged from participating in any type of active recreation.

Women have played sports at various times and places throughout the world, for varying reasons. Sports historian Allen Guttmann reports that girls in the Diola tribe in Gambia historically participated in wrestling matches as a rite of passage, that Native American girls and women played sports that were courtship and fertility rituals, and that Spartan women were expected to demonstrate their skills as wrestlers and to pursue physical fitness just as men did. (Guttmann, 8-15) The classical myth of Atalanta, popular among the Greeks and Romans, deserves mention here: she was unbeatable by men in footraces until one of them stooped to cheating. Even the poor Greek women who were banned from watching the Olympics, much less participating in them, who could not show their faces in the gymnasia, participated in games to celebrate the goddess Hera. The Heraia was for women what the Olympics were for men. (Guttmann, 23) Guttmann points out that there are historical references to women playing sports in imperial Rome and to female gladiators from Ethiopia. Folk football, akin to rugby or soccer, was a popular game for women in the Middle Ages. Stoolball, a game similar to baseball, was also played mostly by women. In 1427, Margot of Hainault defeated all the men at a tennis match in Paris. (Guttmann, 39 - 48) And there are historical references to female bullfighters in Spain and depictions of women participating with men in the sport of bullbaiting. (Guttmann, 59) Thus, there have always been times and places when and where women could and did participate in sports, even contact sports, although these opportunities were by no means universal.

Some contact sports have a long history of being played by women although few people (including athletes who play the sport) are aware of this history. For instance, women in Canada and some parts of the United States have always played ice hockey. More than one hundred years ago, in 1892, a number of all-women hockey teams played each other in an exhibition style touring league. By the 1920s, there were hundreds of women's teams playing hockey. But after two world wars and one Great Depression, the opportunities for women to play hockey all but disappeared; hockey soon became a men-only sport and women were discouraged from playing. It would be the 1980s before female hockey players began to re-emerge in any significant numbers and the 1990s before girls' youth leagues became common. (Theberge)

In the 1920s, the NFL used women's teams to entertain the spectators at halftime. (Kantor) In the early 1930s, two Toledo women's tackle football teams played exhibition games throughout the Midwest. Although financially successful, the experiment was met with considerable opposition and disapproval. The teams were disbanded when Lou Henry Hoover

(Mrs. Herbert Hoover) sent a letter accusing the organizers of "exploiting womanhood." ("Girls Football") Again, the Great Depression and a world war prevented further female forays into football; it became male-only turf.

Interest in women's football was revived forty years later. In the 1970s, a number of women's football teams were organized, mostly on the West Coast and in Canada. Reading the roster of players, one has to admire their tenacity—they certainly didn't have a lot of size. One running back topped the scales at 105 pounds, while a defensive tackled weighed in at a whopping 150. Many of these teams were part of the National Women's Football League. Franchise names give a clue as to how these teams were promoted: the Tucson (AZ) Wild Kittens, the Tulsa Babes, the Los Angeles Scandals, the Chicago Sirens. Some of their games were televised locally, although attendance figures were low—900 spectators for one game was considered typical. Financial problems plagued the teams. They suffered from little publicity and had almost no fan base. In short, they were not taken seriously. Most teams folded after only a year or two. Intermittent attempts to start women's football teams continued throughout the next 20 years.

In 1999, another women's professional football league began playing games, but financial problems again caused the league to falter. In August 2000, the National Women's Football League began playing exhibition games with two teams—the Nashville Dream and the Alabama Renegades. Its regular season runs from mid-March through June. (National Women's Football League website)

Overseas, women's professional football leagues have fared slightly better. In 1986, the American Football Verband Deutschland (American Football Association of Germany) formed women's teams. In Australia, pro women's teams began playing in 1987. Both leagues are still in operation. (Kantor)

That women have played contact sports for decades comes as news to most people. Given the lack of publicity about women in sports in general, it is not surprising that people believe women have never participated in contact sports, at least not before 1995, when the Golden Gloves began sanctioning boxing matches between female amateurs. But in the past few years, a startling development has occurred in the mainstream press: sportswriters and other journalists are beginning to take note of women who participate in contact sports. These sports include certain martial arts, such as Tae Kwon Do and karate, in which participants spar with varying degrees of contact; boxing, in which participants attempt to knock each other out; ice hockey, in which participants manage to bruise each other even if actual fights are prohibited; wrestling, in which participants try to pin each other to the mat; and even football and rugby, in which participants—well, in which participants smash into each other with the intent of making the opponent give ground.

Who are the women who play contact sports? They include Tonya Butler, who wants to be the first woman to play in a Division I college football game; Laila Ali, a professional boxer who wants to follow in her father's footsteps; Margaret MacGregor, the first woman to fight a man in a professional boxing bout (she won); and Manon Rheume, a goalie who become the first woman to play in a hockey game in the National Hockey League.

Although these women are interested in being "first" to do something, women have always participated in contact sports —just not in any significant numbers and without any press coverage. That women have participated in contact sports for some years doesn't mean the idea of women in these sports is accepted or considered acceptable by most people. The so-called Title IX regulations, which are supposed to guarantee equal opportunity for female college students, and which are generally invoked to assure gender equity on the playing field, have nothing to say about women who want to participate in contact sports. If a college wishes to prohibit women from playing contact sports, it can do so, as long as it allows them the opportunity to play other sports. Most college athletic directors can't give a good reason why women shouldn't participate in contact sports, they just prohibit it. Some colleges have women's rugby teams and similar sports; none embrace the idea of co-ed participation in contact sports. While women on women-only teams playing contact sports elicits some disapproval, the idea of men and women playing contact sports together causes the most resistance. And not just among university administrators.

Officials with boxing organizations called the MacGregor match a "sideshow" that "sets back the sport." According to a *Sports Illustrated* article covering the match, "many people think male-female boxing crosses a line that shouldn't be crossed." Male-female boxing isn't the only co-ed sport that is seen as "crossing a line that shouldn't be crossed." Indeed, as recently as August of 1999, Olympic hockey player (and gold medalist) Angela Ruggiero was kicked off a public hockey rink when she tried to play in a game with men.

It isn't just co-ed contact sports that observers disapprove of. Plenty of people think that women in any contact sport, simply playing against each other, also crosses a line that shouldn't be crossed. Consider sportswriter Leigh Montville's attack on women's boxing as "a sick athletic cartoon." He claims that women participating in contact sports are being exploited. (This argument is frequently used to protect women from making choices for themselves.)

The women involved don't seem to think they are being exploited. "This is a dream of mine," says Freeda Foreman, the daughter of boxing legend George Foreman. "I want to let women know there are no limitations. ("Falling in Line") Laila Ali says, "I just love how it feels." ("Another Ali")

As female participation in violent sports such as boxing, hockey, and martial arts grows, so do the questions. Women who play contact sports can no longer be called a "novelty" or a "gimmick," as they have been in the past. So why do women participate in violent sports, and what does it mean?

That's what PUNCH! Why Women Participate in Violent Sports seeks to explore. The book includes my personal experience, plus the experiences—and explanations—of other women in contact sports, some of them well known, some of them not, all of them defying traditional gender roles. Through research and interviews with athletes, coaches, and observers, the reasons why women participate in contact sports—and what they get out of them—is examined. The "violent" sports I refer to are contact sports. Non-contact sports, such as hunting, might also be considered violent (especially if you are the deer), but they are not within the scope of this book. Contact sports included in the book are some types of martial arts, which have contact sparring (even if it is light contact) as a principle part of training; wrestling; tackle football (the kind played by Americans); rugby; and, after due deliberation, ice hockey, which, even with a no-checking policy in the women's leagues, is a rough game. One athlete felt that polo should be considered a contact sport, "in which," she points out, "there is a significant amount of checking (like hockey but with about 1200 pounds of horse along with you)." (Torrance) But I will have to save polo for another book. Readers might argue why I included one sport (ice hockey) and not another (lacrosse) that could as easily be considered a contact sport. The short answer is that most people recognize the sports that I have included and understand, in essence, at least, how they are played and would agree that they are contact sports. The even shorter answer is that there are many more women playing these contact sports than there are playing sports such as lacrosse. Having access to women playing a specific contact sport was a consideration when I began to research and write this book. Thus, since I had dozens of hockey players respond to my requests for information and had exactly one lacrosse player respond, I crossed lacrosse off and put hockey in. It would certainly be of interest to learn more about women in the less-well-known contact sports, but that is not the primary purpose of this book.

*PUNCH! Why Women Participate in Violent Sports* attempts to describe not only the fact of women punching, but *why* women want to punch in the first place.

# *Chapter One:*
# Why Now?

It is hard to imagine how much sports for women were still in the dark ages when I was growing up. Hard to imagine because it wasn't so very long ago. Title IX was officially passed in 1972, when I was 7 years old, although it would be many more years before women and sports would feel its effects in an insistent, positive way. I didn't even hear of Title IX until I was 27, that's how much of an effect it had on my life, on the lives of women my age. I first learned about Title IX from a woman whose husband coached college basketball, and she had nothing good to say about it. Title IX, as Amendment IX of the Civil Rights Act has come to be called, mandated that all educational institutions that received federal funds had to provide equal opportunity to both sexes in all programs. It had an unforeseen effect on athletic programs when school officials realized that they had to bring sports programs into compliance with the new law. (Zimmerman 13) Title IX would have an effect on the women who came after me, on women like my nearly 10 years younger sister, who played softball and tennis and soccer on school teams. (See Appendix for complete text of Title IX legislation.) But it took many years for women to benefit from this legislation, and even now it is not consistently enforced and followed. Nonetheless, it helped many people, even non-athletes, think about what we mean by gender equity and what we want from it.

I was among the last generation of women who grew up believing that women were weak and frail and had to be protected, that strenuous exertion could harm women in ways it could not harm men, that a woman could never be the physical equal (let alone superior) of any man. And in 1992, when I walked into the training hall for the first time, I was just beginning to learn that everything I believed was wrong.

I was one of a wave of women in the 1990s who looked around at the opportunities and decided that a contact sport appealed to them. Although women have participated in violent sports for many years, only recently have large numbers of women begun punching and kicking, and only recently has there been mainstream media attention focused on them.

Why now? What drew us to the gyms, the rings, the training halls? What did we have to wait for?

A number of factors contributed to this surge of interest in contact sports by women. Some of these factors are obvious—there are more women now than ever interested in sports—any sports. They watch them and they play them. In the last few decades, changing ideas of gender roles have encouraged women to see themselves involved in sports, whereas in the past they were encouraged to stay on the sidelines and cheer. In addition, the fitness movement of the 1980s encouraged girls and women to play sports as a means of getting into shape. Certain legal requirements—such as Title IX—have encouraged schools at all levels to support women's sports programs. And adult women are starting to realize that the things they couldn't do when they were children—the things they were not allowed to do—were now available to them. If you're 10 and your mother won't let you play on the boys' hockey team, that's one thing. If you're 30, and you want to play on the boys' hockey team, it doesn't really matter what your mother wants.

Further, with women demanding more equality in the workplace, there is a concomitant tendency toward demanding equality on the playing field. Men and women alike are more attuned to disparities that exist between opportunities for men and women. And there are more women spectators and sportswriters who help draw attention to women's participation in sports. Women are also, slowly, seeking more positions in coaching, administration and refereeing. A few years ago, the NBA hired several seasoned referees, who happened to be female. Although many of the male basketball players criticized the move, the women have continued to work alongside male referees with few problems. Such strides have convinced more women to take an active interest in sports and to imagine possibilities in sports once their active playing days are over.

Feminist thinkers and activists have challenged ideas about what it means to be a woman, although, as the feminist scholar Martha McCaughey points out, "Unfortunately, however, their books have appeared remote from the concerns (and vernacular) of everyday women." Nonetheless, some of this thinking has filtered down to the "everyday" world where women use it to justify seeking the same opportunities as men, in all arenas.

More immediate to everyday women are media images that have begun to portray women as strong, even violent. In films, movies and television shows, women are being shown more often (although by no means frequently) as the aggressor—the films *Terminator 2* and *Thelma and Louise* spring to mind. "These media images," McCaughey says, "offer new fantasies of what women can be, which rests on women's abilities to set boundaries, defend themselves and enter into combat."

For me, it was *Lethal Weapon 3*, which showed a female protagonist who could match Mel Gibson scar for scar, and who could perform martial arts techniques as well as he could. Other women in contact sports acknowledge the impact of media images on their choices. These new images are not going away soon. Movies featuring women in contact sports, such as *Girlfight* and *Shadow Boxers* were released in 2000. In 2001 *Crouching Tiger, Hidden Dragon*, won several awards and featured almost solely women fighting each other. It is likely that other movies and shows about women in contact sports will be filmed and screened in the coming years.

In addition, corporate interest in women's sports has increased. Corporations now sponsor and advertise women's competitions. At least five new magazines designed for female athletes have hit newsstands in the last few years. And companies have finally gotten around to designing athletic gear that real women can wear to work out in (not those spandex unitards). Sporting goods companies have realized that not all women who work out do aerobics and that not all women who work out wear a size eight. Recent strides in gear include sports bras for fuller figured women, chest and groin protectors specifically designed for women in contact sports, wrestling singlets for girls and women, even bag gloves and boxing gloves designed to fit women's smaller hands. (Zimmerman, 15 - 16)

In terms of sheer numbers, women are substantially more involved in sports now than they were a generation ago. According to studies conducted to determine the impact of Title IX on women in sports, in 1970 one in every 27 high school girls played school sports; now, one in three do. Almost 2½ million girls play school sports, as compared to about three million boys. Title IX, which has been called a "notorious legal hammer" in the mainstream press, requires colleges to fund men's and women's sports equally. Colleges must provide an equal number of roster sports "on the theory," as one commentator expresses it, "that having fewer openings sends the message that women are not expected to play sports." (Menard, 87)

In a classic case often cited to prove the pervasive effect of Title IX, in 1991 Brown University reduced four teams, including women's gymnastics, to club status, meaning the university no longer provided financial support for them. The gymnasts sued. Although Brown had 16 sports for men and 16 sports for women, 62% of varsity athletes were men and only 38% were women (the student body is comprised of roughly equal numbers of men and women). The university claimed to provide opportunities for women but that more men wanted to play sports. The gymnasts called this attitude "the kind of sexist thinking that Title IX was designed to remedy." The university's official line reflected the perception that women don't like sports, which is demonstrably not true. The First Circuit Court agreed with the gymnasts. The university was required to not only support women's teams, but to recruit women to play on them. (Menard, 87) Each year, colleges and universities try to find ways to get out of funding men and women's sports equally, and each year, women have to sue. But at least the legislation that is in place allows them to.

In addition to these achievements that have helped push forward the cause of women's sports, certain commercial and sporting venues have helped to highlight women's achievements in sports. Observers agree that the Atlanta Olympics in 1996 showcased the talents of female athletes to great effect: who can forget the image of Kerri Strug in the arms of her coach? The Nagano Winter Olympics in 1998 also showed how tough and strong women could be when Picabo Street, after enduring several serious injuries the previous year, won the downhill gold. The American women's ice hockey team also won gold, and, to cap off the festivities, the International Olympic Committee agreed that no additional sports would be added to the roster of Olympic sports unless they could be played by both men and women. (Zimmerman, 10)

In 1999, the Women's World Cup soccer tournament drew nearly 100,000 spectators to the championship game. When the American team won in a shoot-out, practically every little girl in America was watching and wanted to learn how to play the game—if she wasn't already playing.

In 2000, a record number of women competed in the Sydney Summer Olympics. More than 3900 women entered these Olympics of a total of just over 10,000 competitors, meaning they comprised slightly less than 40% of all participants. A contact sport, Tae Kwon Do, was added to the Olympics; both men and women competed.

Progress in women's sports has been helped by organizations such as the Women's Sports Foundation, which was established in 1974 to encourage women to participate in athletics and to support their goals. The executive director of the foundation, Donna Lopiano, says, "The function of the Women's Sports Foundation is to be the impatient, intolerant voice of women's sports. ...I wish in my lifetime I could see no need for the Women's Sports Foundation." ("Out of the Shadows: Foundation still fighting for rights of female athletes")

Even seemingly minor factors such as rules changes have also helped women get involved in sports, especially contact sports. A school wrestling coach says simply, "Girls didn't go out for wrestling when we had a hair code." (Anderson) The hair code was straightforward: hair had to be worn above the ears in a buzz cut. Safety reasons were cited: if hair were worn longer, competitors could grab each other's hair and possibly inflict injury. But the code also reflected the unexpressed belief that only boys would wrestle anyway. Wearing their hair like this was not appealing to many girls or women—especially since, as novices, they weren't even sure if they would enjoy wrestling. The hair code was like a barrier to entry that few women would care to surmount. After a lawsuit by religious groups (a Native American male wrestler challenged the rule and was supported by several organizations), the hair code was changed so that people could have longer hair if they tucked it into a cap worn under the headgear. After this rule change, Coach Anderson says, "lots of girls started going out for wrestling." Other important rules changes have allowed girls and women to participate on formerly all-boys' or all-men's teams, especially in cases where a girls' team is not available.

Because of gender equity laws, women are using the courts to have their day on the courts. In the mid-80s, Justine Blainey had to sue to join a boys' hockey team she had successfully tried out for. She would have joined a girls' team, she said. If there had been one .(Theberge, 150) In 1993, then 16-year-old boxer Dallas Malloy sued the U.S. Amateur Boxing Federation for the right to compete in title fights. (Zimmerman, 196) Both suits were successful. Blainey was allowed to skate and Mallory was allowed to fight. Previously, girls and women who wanted to play contact sports could simply be barred from doing so, and they would have no legal remedy. Legislation in the last 30 years has helped changed this, and girls and women are not afraid to confront entrenched bias in sports in order to play their games.

Another important factor in the increasing participation of girls and women in sports is that for the first time, a future is emerging for some athletes. With the advent of the women's professional basketball league, the Women's National Basketball Association, young female basketball players are starting to feel that perhaps they could become professionals. Just like little boys grow up thinking they could be like Mike, little girls are starting to grow up thinking they could be like Leslie, or

Chamique, or other professional basketball players who happen to be women. The WNBA, affiliated with the NBA, was established in 1996, shortly after the American Basketball League (another women's basketball league) began operations. The ABL later dissolved.

Other professional leagues, including ice hockey and football, have been launched with uneven success. Still, girls and women who enjoy playing sports are starting to believe that they could continue their participation past puberty, or past college, and have some reward for doing so. Although you can practically hear the reluctance by the male-dominated sporting world, openings in coaching, administration, sports journalism and league organization have yielded to women who have spent their lives playing sports. Others are eager to follow in their footsteps.

Slowly but surely these changes have encouraged girls and women to compete in sports. The National Collegiate Athletics Association, the organization that administers college sports, reported that athletic scholarships to women in the 1997-1998 academic year had increased more than 140 percent since the 1991-1992 school year. While men continued to receive the lion's share of scholarships and funding, the gap had narrowed considerably and the number of women competing in Division I sports had risen to 40% of the total number of athletes. Compliance still has a considerable length to travel before true parity exists, but improvements are marked each year, although some observers, even those in the NCAA, believe that progress is much slower than it could be. ("Narrowing the Gap: NCAA reports number of female athletes up to 40%")

While all of these factors might explain why women participate in sports more now than in the past, it doesn't explain why they participate in contact sports—violent sports, if you will. In the 1990s, as journalist Colette Dowling (*The Frailty*

*Myth*) says, women "plung[ed] victoriously into the contact sports—ice hockey, football, rugby—for so long considered ineffably 'male.'" (35)

Is this truly a trend? Are there really that many female competitors in contact sports? The answer is an unequivocal yes. More than one thousand female football players have found places on high school and college football teams. Most are kickers, but some are running backs or defensive players. In the fall of 1999, Katie Hnida, a kicker, became the first woman to suit up for a Big 12 game when her school, Colorado, played Kansas (Heys). Highland Community College in Topeka, Kansas, sponsored a football camp for girls in the summer of 1999 and filled all its slots. "Now that I have references," said one participant, "I feel more comfortable asking for the chance" to play on her junior high football team. (Albright)

The Golden Gloves Association sanctioned women's amateur boxing in 1995, allowing women to gain official ring experience. In the years since the Golden Gloves began sanctioning women's amateur matches, more than 2000 women have registered as amateur boxers (and countless others box or train to box but not in sanctioned bouts). This sparked an avalanche of interest in *professional* women's boxing—now, over 700 women are professional boxers, with scores more making their professional boxing debuts each year. The pay day isn't much, but it is professional women's boxing, something unheard of just a decade ago.

In the fall of 1999, the Women's Professional Football League debuted. Players from all over the country tried out for two teams—the Minnesota Vixens and the Lake Michigan Minx—that participated in the "No Limits" exhibition tour. In 2000-2001, a total of 11 teams were organized and played a short season. Although they gave up jobs, left their families and traveled on their own dimes, the women football players saw it as a chance to establish that women can play contact sports and draw a crowd. That the crowd was mostly men titillated by the thought of women hitting each other seemed irrelevant to the players. They simply hoped that eventually their skills, not their gender, would be their drawing card, and that they would be able to help the league flourish. Until now, professional football has remained closed to women, and these players seemed eager for the chance to make a mark. When a reporter told them the league couldn't possibly work, the women responded, "But it was really fun." (Dohrmann, "Full Contact," 27)

Sadly, as reported by *Sports Illustrated* in early 2001, "the much-touted women's pro football league is in shambles" with disorganized and canceled road trips, unpaid bills and lack of equipment. "Who knows what the WPFL, if it is around, will look like next season?" says Jodi Armstrong, a fullback for the Minnesota Vixens. Nonetheless, in 2000 Catherine Masters, a marketing executive, started the National Women's Football League with two teams competing in exhibition games. Over the next few seasons, she expects the league to expand to eight to twelve teams. (Dohrmann, "Girl Trouble")

Clearly, many women are attracted to playing contact sports. It is not just a handful of tough cookies, a few hardy women who defy gender conventions, break all the rules, and play a sport that leaves them with bruises. It is hundreds of women. *Thousands* of them. Why?

Some experts speculate that women have begun to participate in contact sports as a means of pushing the envelope, so to speak, to determine how far they can go. Among female athletes in contact sports, there is an almost universal rebellious streak. They say, in essence, "You can't tell me what to do."

But they continually run into people who do want to tell them what to do. And one of the things they want to tell them to do is to quit playing contact sports. Up until now, "touch among teammates and between opponents [has been] a right (and rite) of manhood." (Cahn, 222) When women intrude on that territory, they threaten male turf. Perhaps this is one reason why some men seem determined to scare them off.

In the fall of 1999, Angela Ruggiero, a member of the women's ice hockey team that had just won gold at the Olympics, "wandered into a public rink... carrying her skates and sticks, looking for a pickup game. Sorry, she was told. She couldn't play. ...The reason: a men-only rule. In this rink, the gals couldn't play with the guys, regardless of who had the gold medal and who didn't." ("Out of the Shadows: Foundation still fighting for rights of female athletes")

The owners of the rink were soon reminded that gender discrimination is against the law. But it hasn't always been so. In the past, Ruggiero wouldn't have had any recourse if she wanted to play with men. Even if she is better than they are.

In 1999, Heather Sue Mercer sued Duke University and ex-football coach Fred Goldsmith, claiming she was discriminated against under the regulations set forth by Title IX. The Fourth US Circuit Court of Appeals ruled, contrary to a lower court ruling, that Title IX does not require single-sex contact sports (such as football) to allow members of the opposite sex to try out, *but* if a school does allow members of both genders to try out, then it must treat all participants fairly. An attorney for Heather Sue Mercer explained the ruling this way: "Once you've invited her to participate on the team, you can't treat her as a second-class citizen." Mercer had alleged that her exclusion from the team was because of her gender. (Levy)

A place-kicker for her high school all-state team, Mercer was first exposed to the glare of media attention in 1995, when she kicked the game-winning field goal during the Blue-White scrimmage game at Duke University. Afterward, Coach Goldsmith told her (and everyone else, including the media) that she had made the team. Later, he reneged. Mercer alleged that Goldsmith did not allow her to participate in practice or to wear a uniform and later told her to sit in the stands with her boyfriend during games. Nonetheless, Mercer continued to participate in training, both in endurance and in kicking exercises. (Levy)

Goldsmith worsened his case by telling her to give up "little boys' sports," to try beauty pageants or cheerleading. Eventually, he banned her from the sidelines. He also told reporters how pretty she was, as if that were relevant to her football skills. She was the first team member he cut, keeping a male kicker who was not as accomplished. (Levy)

Although university officials were confident they would succeed in proving that Mercer was not a victim of discrimination, but instead was simply a poor place kicker, Mercer eventually won her lawsuit. In October 2000, a jury awarded her $2 million in punitive damages. Unfortunately, it may be that other women won't get the chance to try out; the court pointed out that allowing her to try out in the first place had allowed the discrimination charge to proceed. If the university had continued its ban on allowing women to try out, discrimination could not have been found. ("Woman Placekicker's Lawsuit: Blue Devil of a Time")

This resistance to women in contact sports goes deep in the culture. Women are still routinely banned from participating in traditionally single-sex contact sports, even when they don't necessarily want to play on mixed gender teams.

This is true outside the United States as well. In November, 2000, Dierdre Nelson was forced to sue the Boxing Union of Ireland (BUI) for a license to box in Ireland. The holder of a British boxing license, Nelson claims the BUI has denied her the right to fight based solely on her gender. At the time of this writing, the case had not been resolved. (Women's Boxing Page)

The answer frequently given for why there is such a deep-seated resistance to women in contact sports is straightforward: it is not considered gender appropriate. That is, real women don't punch each other. Nonetheless, women are stretching the bounds of what is considered gender appropriate. Although contact sports have not been considered gender appropriate for women, those sports that *are* considered acceptable for women has proven to be very fluid in the past. In her book, *Coming on Strong*, historian Susan K. Cahn points out that basketball was considered gender appropriate for women when it was first invented late in the nineteenth century. It was played indoors, there was little physical contact between players and speed and power were not as important as technical accuracy. Later, basketball was appropriated by male players and female players were discouraged from playing—lacking, according to prevailing belief, the necessary skills to play a game they had previously been thought to have exactly the right skills to play. Only recently has the game seemed appropriate for women again, although they play it according to slightly different rules than men do. (85)

Cahn goes on to point out that prior to the 1950s, gymnastics was considered a very male sport. Only later did it become a more "feminine sport." (221) Further back in time, sports historian Allen Guttmann reports, medieval women played folk football (a game similar to rugby or soccer). By the Renaissance, folk football more closely resembled soccer, was less physical, and was played by upper class men. (57)

What sports are considered gender appropriate, then, change over time. Women are beginning to cross the boundary of "gender appropriate" behavior to pursue contact sports without worrying if it compromises them as women. But what is gender appropriate is also a function of social class, sports historian Guttmann contends. Historically, he points out, women of the lower classes wrestled and boxed. Middle class women pursued leisure activities such as walking and tennis, while upper class women hunted. Only in the past few years have these social distinctions faded and has it become more acceptable for women from all backgrounds to play the entire spectrum of sports, including contact sports. (2)

But the common perception still holds that women and girls "don't play contact sports, especially football." (Zimmerman, 194) In 1997, Liz Heaston became the first woman to play NCAA football. Now, nearly 1000 girls play football in more than 70 high school football programs. Partly this is owing to a lack of male participants, which means that coaches are willing to consider female players; partly it is owing to changing attitudes about gender roles. What it means, essentially, is that our ideas about what is a "gender appropriate" sport are changing. As a culture, we are coming to accept that some contact sports might be gender appropriate for women. One athlete speaks for many women when she says,"Excellence knows no gender." (Torrance)

The situation is somewhat different outside the United States. Each country addresses the question of gender equity differently; since gender is culturally defined, it is only natural that each cultural grapples with its definition differently.

"There is no Title IX in Britain," says one rugby player. There, she says, women being viewed as second-class athletes is "treated as normal. I couldn't imagine that in the States." (Uzelac) In Europe, women's sports teams are still called "ladies'" teams. However, most European countries have implemented programs to provide needed impetus to encourage the participation of women and girls in sports. To a lesser degree, Asian and African countries are pursuing these goals as well.

In 1994, an international conference on women and sport, organized by the British Sports Council and endorsed by the

International Olympic Committee, was held in Brighton, UK. At this time, the Brighton Declaration was adapted in order to speed the process of change in providing equality for women involved in sports. Representatives from 82 countries and numerous sports organizations endorsed the declaration and agreed to establish a women and sport strategy that could be adopted worldwide. (See Appendix for complete text of the Brighton Declaration.)

The conference identified key issues: women and girls make up more than 50% of the world population yet their rates of participation in sports are far less than men and boys worldwide. Although more women participate in sports than in the past, they have not achieved increased representation in decision-making and leadership roles. And, finally, women are underrepresented in management, coaching and officiating.

The International Working Group on Women and Sports was formed at this conference in order to coordinate the activities of various governmental and non-governmental organizations in developing opportunities in sports for girls and women. The group has identified five main aims, including overseeing the adoption of the Brighton Declaration worldwide, developing an action plan targeting areas where women and sports are not priorities, facilitating the exchange of information, promoting the inclusion of women and sports issues at major conferences, and sponsoring the 2002 World Conference on Women and Sports. (The International Working Group on Women and Sport website) These ambitious aims will certainly enhance opportunities for girls and women in sports.

Signatories to the Brighton Declaration included numerous government and sports organizations, and included countries as diverse as Algeria, Madagascar, Zimbabwe, Bahrain, Indonesia, Syria, Aruba, Grenada, Argentina, Panama and Papua New Guinea—along with Germany, Switzerland, the

United Kingdom and Canada.

In 1998, a second world conference was held, this time in Windhoek, Namibia. Four hundred representatives from 74 countries established a plan for action to further develop sports opportunities for girls and women. The conference stressed coordination and cooperation among the numerous organizations that address women's issues. (Windhoek Conference) (See Appendix for complete text of the Windhoek Conference Call for Action.) Another world conference is scheduled for May, 2002 in Montreal.

In the United Kingdom, a national action plan was developed by Sport England and the Women's Sports Foundation to answer the needs identified by the two world conferences. The Women's Sports Foundation (WSF), established in 1984, bills itself as "the only organization in the UK that is solely committed to improving and promoting opportunities for women and girls in sport at every level." ("About the WSF")

The WSF promotes the positive influence sports participation has on girls and women and identifies a wide range of barriers to participation. To overcome these barriers, the WSF attempts to increase awareness, to support women and girls in sports, to encourage improved access to sports, to challenge inequality, and to raise the visibility of girls and women in sports. The organization lobbies decision-makers, advises sports providers, encourages research, sponsors training and education programs, helps sportswomen deal with the media and provides fact sheets and information in response to thousands of inquiries each year. ("About the WSF")

Elsewhere in the world, efforts to increase the participation of women in sports have met with varied degrees of success. The Sports Council for Wales has conducted research showing that slightly over 40% of Welsh women participate in sports while more than half of men do. To close the gap, the

Council has redoubled efforts to increase opportunities for women and girls at the grassroots level, to promote women's sports and thereby raise their profile, and to encourage more women to coach. ("Women and Girls")

In Scotland, Sportscotland, an organization dedicated to increasing sporting activity among all citizens, recently reported an increase of women's sports and fitness participation. 59% of Scottish women now regularly participate in some form of fitness activity, compared to 68% for men. The only criticism to be leveled against this remarkable achievement is that games such as bowling, and activities such as walking and birdwatching are considered sporting activity. (Sportscotland website).

The Sports Council for Northern Ireland reports that 53% of women actively participate in sports while 67% of men do. The SCNI has committed to enhancing programs for women and the disabled. Most of the emphasis in these organizations is on involving children and young adult in sports and sports leadership roles. (Sportscotland website)

In 1995, the Women's Sports and Fitness Foundation Malaysia was established as a voluntary organization for promoting fitness and well-being and for providing sports and fitness opportunities for girls and women. The organization was formed because of the rapid development of sports opportunities for women. Ten goals make up the organization's mission, such as efforts to include Malaysian women from all socio-economic classes, to increase awareness of health and fitness, to support research, to organize seminars and conferences, to increase coverage of women's sports in the media, to sponsor the training of women in fields such as coaching, refereeing and administration, and several other related goals. ("Who We Are")

In other parts of the world, organizations dedicated to promoting women and sports have sprung up, including some in the most unlikely places. The more important of these organizations include the Japanese Association for Women and Sport, Arab Women and Sport Association, Asia Women and Sport Association, African Women in Sport Association, Sport Society of Egyptian Women, Women in Sports Foundation Zimbabwe, Indonesian Association of Physical Education and Sports for Girls and Women, Women's Sports Foundation Philippines, and Lithuanian Women in Sport Association. Clearly, the issue of women and sports is achieving attention throughout the world. It remains to be seen what the end result of these efforts will be and if these organizations can provide women with the support and opportunities they need to succeed in sports.

In addition, several international organizations exist to further the development of sports opportunities for girls and women, including WomenSport International and the International Olympic Committee's Women and Sport Working Group. These groups coordinate the efforts of individual national groups and provide resources for chronically underfunded programs.

Certainly, much progress has been made in allowing women and girls more access to sports opportunities. But the question still remains, why would women and girls participate in *contact* sports when they have the opportunity to play other, less dangerous sports? It may be "almost like a revolution," as journalist Jean Zimmerman says, but what started the revolution? (210)

A former pro basketball player, sportswriter Mariah Burton Nelson says, "[Women] are getting pleasure out of sheer physical competence. They are taking physical risks and having fun in the process. ...Sports participation has given millions of women new self-confidence and has taken them where they never were before—onto what used to be male turf." (4)

This idea of taking physical risks is very important to women who participate in contact sports. In a society that encourages women to be afraid, taking physical risks can be very reassuring. Rather than being afraid of getting hurt, they learn that getting hurt doesn't mean the end of the world. The fear of physical pain or injury does not cause them to panic anymore. After you've iced a couple of good bruises, you are much less afraid of getting bruised. You begin to imagine that you are strong, that you are tough, that you are not frail, that you do not need to be protected.

Or at least that has been my experience. Once, I got slammed to the floor when an unskilled partner threw me during takedown practice. I later learned that I had broken my arm in two places. At the time I just knew it hurt. But that didn't stop me from continuing the training session or from sparring three or four different partners before the end of the session. The next day, my arm still swollen, I visited my doctor and saw the x-rays that showed what an impact fracture looks like. It didn't matter to me that I'd broken my arm—you expect you're going to get an injury now and then when you play a contact sport—except that now I wasn't going to be able to train as hard as usual until my arm healed. The fact that I had continued to train for the rest of the session didn't mean anything special about me—most players in contact sports have stories of playing while injured.

Do I think this is an especially healthy attitude to have? No. But I recognized then, as I do now, that you can get hurt and you can keep on going. That fear and pain, while they exist, don't have to stop you. That while you might never be impervious to fear, you can at least *act* like you are impervious to it. For me, breaking my arm and continuing to spar meant that I didn't have to be afraid of pain of injury, afraid of what someone could do to me. I could be hurt, in pain, sick, and I could still fight back. Women are hardly ever encouraged to learn that about themselves. As journalist Jean Zimmerman says, "people underestimate how much girls [and women] want to feel strong." (209)

When I broke my arm and kept going, I felt strong. I *knew* I was strong. A rugby player says, "After the first game, I learned that they had all placed bets on how long I would last. No one dreamt I would make it and stick with it. ...I broke my hand in the first game I played and played through the whole game before [asking] to go to the E.R. I won respect from them at that time. I guess they figured I was not a cheerleader." (Park)

Other women agree on the importance of feeling strong and tough—a feeling that only contact sports can give them. One woman says, "Is hockey mean? Is hockey rough and tumble? Absolutely, and what better way is there to vent all the daily stresses we endure?" (Wiechers)

A martial artist concurs: "I found a part of me I didn't know existed. I *liked* being 'tough.' I could get out angers I was holding in, in an acceptable way. I could hit as hard as I could, kick as hard as I could, throw every bit of anger into my moves and it was acceptable. The release of pent up emotions was exhilarating, to say the least. It was a true sense of euphoria." (Troutwine)

For some, the exhilaration of physical contact does not have to be enjoyed in the guise of venting stress, however. Another hockey player agrees that feeling tough is important: "I do love feeling strong, powerful, when you take somebody out in front of the net," she says, but she doesn't say anything about the physical contact being a means of venting stress. Instead, she says, "The physical aspect of hockey, while it is the most grueling, is the most satisfying. Waking up the next day, bruised and aching from head to foot, makes me feel as if I really did something, I gave everything I had in that game, and I was a success even if we lost as a team." (Wellman)

For her, toughness and physical exertion combine to create personal success (success that is, interestingly enough, independent of the team's performance). Feeling spent and exhausted is a measure of how much of herself she gave to the game. If she comes up short, she is not a success, she is not tough enough.

Spending oneself on the playing field as a measure of success is a theme emphasized by others in contact sports. A football player comments, "I enjoy playing football. There is a lot of contact and there have been times I did not think I was going to be able to get up off the ground. But I continue to play the sport for the love of playing competitively and for the sport itself." (Walsh) Contact sports appeal to us in a way that non-contact sports—even competitive non-contact sports—never can.

As women continue to make strides in all areas of their lives—in their careers, in their relationships—they learn that there are no predetermined limits to what they can do. They challenge previously held opinions about what's good for them, about what goals they can pursue, and what it means to be successful. For all these reasons, and more, women who want to push themselves, to learn what they can do, are taking up contact sports.

## Chapter Two
# How Women Get Involved

Ali, Foreman and Frazier are all names familiar to fight fans. But the first names of these fighters might not be so familiar: Laila, Freeda, Jacqui. That's right. The *daughters* of the most famous boxers in history are taking up their gloves and stepping into the ring. More than 700 women are registered as professional boxers in the United States. More than 2,000 are registered amateurs. Just a few years ago, there were none. How on earth did they get involved in fighting? Where did they come from?

Say you have a famous father who used to box. Maybe you grew up in the gym, listening to the slap of the speed bag and the thwack of the jump rope. Makes a certain amount of sense that you might want to follow in Dad's footsteps. But what if you didn't grow up in the gym? How on earth would you get there?

When Laila Ali got knocked down in her fifth professional fight—her first fight that wasn't against a powder puff opponent—her manager and fiancé Johnny McClain said, "Laila got up and did her thing. She's a true warrior." (St. Jorre, 110) You hardly ever hear that woman are warriors. It has a nice sound, one that appeals to plenty of women, not just boxers.

The women who like the sound the best are the women who play contact sports.

But most women who begin playing contact sports don't necessarily have toughness in the mind when they start. Laila Ali recounts the incident that led to her decision to study boxing. When she was 18, she saw two women boxing on television. It was the first time she'd seen women box. "I thought, 'Oh my God, I can do that!'" she says. (St. Jorre, 111) Like many women, she first viewed her training as a form of exercise and only later realized she was interested in the sport as a sport. Jean Martin, a New York City detective, and the number 2-ranked female boxer in the United States, says she started training in 1997 after reading a flier that said, "lose weight, learn how to box." ("Spotlight: Jean Martin, Boxer") Jean, who considered herself overweight, just wanted to get into shape, but then watched the 1997 Golden Gloves and decided she, too, wanted to fight. Now, she says she has told her trainer: "Train me harder than you have ever trained anybody. I have to win." ("Spotlight: Jean Martin, Boxer")

Many women participate in sports in order to get in shape, to lose weight, to make themselves more attractive; only after they've been involved for a while do they see other benefits of their participation in sports. This reason for starting a sport is so prevalent that to this day, when people interview me about my participation in martial arts, they ask me how much weight I lost after I started. As the feminist scholar Martha McCaughey points out, "Women are assessed more for their looks than for their physical abilities." (42) I sense that my interviewers would be disappointed if I told them I had gained weight after starting martial arts training, even if that extra weight made me stronger or a better martial artist.

A kung fu practitioner says she started training because she "thought it would be fun, a good discipline, and an excellent sort of physical training." (Goudsmit) A Tae Kwon Do practitioner says, "It increases my self-confidence, strength and flexibility. It also helps to keep me in shape." (Bove) One martial artist who was thirty-nine when she started training says, "I had had three babies within six years so I was feeling very flabby and run down. When my husband mentioned he was going to enroll himself and our then seven-year-old son in the local Tae Kwon Do school, I jumped at the chance to work out." (Cox)

Although getting fit is often a motivating factor for women who take up contact sports—and there is nothing wrong with that—marketers have jumped on the bandwagon and tout sports as the magic bullet for all one's weigth loss woes. Where once sports were marketed to women as a way to make friends, get fit and have fun, they are now marketed as a means to become thin and to acquire the sexy look beloved of males. (Cahn 176)

Even though this is in some ways discouraging—do we really need more emphasis on weight loss and our appeal to men or lack thereof?—it also means that women can imagine participating in sports without having to give up their femininity, what makes them women. They can participate in sports and still have dates with men. This makes sports more appealing, especially for younger women who are usually influenced by social pressures to a greater degree than older women are. There are some drawbacks to this relationship of sport and attractiveness to men, however, which will be discussed later in the book.

For women who do not say that getting fit was their primary reason for taking up a contact sport, the majority were drawn to contact sports when they learned that a friend played a contact sport. That they knew someone who boxed or wrestled or kicked made the sports seem less intimidating. It also made their own interest seem suddenly acceptable. A hockey player says, "I started to play when a woman I worked with... saw an ad in the paper announcing the start of a woman's team and that they were looking for players." (Formosa) As simple as that, she embarked on a journey of learning and growing to love a contact sport that she had not played before.

A social worker who practices martial arts describes one of the people she worked with: "I admired this social worker. She was young and working in the same field that I wanted to work in. She said karate was a great stress reliever for her, so I thought I would give it a try." (Stambaugh) In this case, the main attraction to the sport was that it represented a new way of being a woman for a young adult unsure of what kind of woman she wanted to be.

The number of women who started playing a contact sport as a matter of timing or coincidence is truly astonishing. One hockey player recounts her start this way:

*After becoming a mom, I met a woman hockey player at a work party for my husband (she had begun playing in her 40s). She told me about a class, which I decided to take. (The only other sport I had tried after the birth of my twins was water aerobics, and hockey sure beats the hell out of that.) After taking the class in the summer of '98 ... a group of women in Lansing formed a team, the Capital Crush (which I joined).* (Schimanski-Gross)

She is not the only one who got her start through an off-hand comment. A football player says simply, "Through a friend I heard about the league. ...They needed players. I showed up at a game and have been playing ever since." (Walsh)

In addition to the casual nature of their initial involvement, what is striking—and important—about the experiences of these women is that it was the establishment of a women-friendly environment, such as a women's team, that got them started. One woman says that when she was 15, "I started playing when a girls' [hockey] team was formed in the area. I had always watched hockey, skated on the rink we had in our backyard, and dreamed of playing... I never really thought I'd have a chance to play competitively." (Kangas, G.) It is clear that she wouldn't have been interested in playing on a boys' team. And she is not the only young woman who got her start because there was finally an opportunity for her to play. Thus, for many women, timing meets opportunity—and they start playing a contact sport.

This is not to overlook the importance of peer influence on women's involvement in contact sports. One hockey player says that after her second child was born, she felt she needed some activity to do and learned that men at her place of work were organizing an ice hockey team. She joined, becoming the only woman on the team—and indeed the only woman in the league. (Lentz) A football player says, "A friend at work was looking for a team sport to join. She decided on football, and it sounded like fun." (Noah) She adds, "I never thought I could play it outside of childhood because I'm a woman."

While some people learn about a sport opportunity through friends or co-workers, many look to family members for inspiration. A hockey player says:

*My older brother played. ...I also remember being the only girl playing. I used to beg my sister to go over to the rink and join in the games with me; once I was involved with the game, I didn't mind if she left. But I never wanted to go over by myself and try to join in as the only girl.* (Hallada-Pinhey)

A rugby player says, "I wanted a new sport. I had done gymnastics all my life. I was looking for something new. My sister played, and it looked like so much fun! Plus, I loved tackling and being tough... or at least feeling tough." (Fancy)

Another hockey player says:

*My brother Ryan, who is four years younger, had always wanted to play hockey. ... When we moved, [my parents]*

27

*decided to let him finally start. ... Since I could skate [friends]*
*double-dared me to give it a try. My parents finally gave in.*
*My father said, 'I will be amazed if you make it through the*
*first half of the season.'* (Ward)

While it is social relationships that often get women involved
in contact sports, it is not uncommon for women to actively
seek out contact sports as a way to meet other people, especially women, who are similar to them. A football player says
she "wanted to connect with other women like me. I had friends
who were academic. I wanted more kinds of friends." She
pauses and adds, "I wanted to explore my masculine side."
(Poehler) The idea that some kinds—that is, *certain* kinds, and
only certain kinds—of people are attracted to contact sports is
echoed by a rugby player, who says rugby was her first team
sport, that she liked the camaraderie and the fact that it "wasn't
something brainy kids did." (Uzelac)

This web of relationships is extremely important, both for
getting women involved in contact sports and keeping them
involved. A hockey coach concurs.

*Most [women] seem to start because they hear of another*
*woman playing. Once they start, they often express that*
*they feel 'hooked.' It's excellent exercise, camaraderie, and*
*the sport itself is addicting in its speed and learning curve.*
*Several women have commented that they 'schlepped' their*
*kid to the rink for years and now they find it's a fun game*
*for them to play, too!"* (McDowell)

About how she herself got started, Coach McDowell says,
"I loved the game since I was a child. ... Always, always, always wanted to be a goalie."

The idea of contact sports as simply something fun to play
is echoed by an 11-year-old girl who plays football with boys
in a recreational league. She says, "It's not fair that only the
boys get to have all the fun." ("Two Girls Suit Up")

There is also an element of deliberate defiance in the choices these women make. Their friends may play a contact sport; they may make friends playing a contact sport; playing a contact sport may be fun, but all of them are perfectly aware that this is not a choice women ordinarily make regardless of how much fun it might be or how many of their friends are involved. They know it defies gender stereotypes and that's fine with them.

A martial artist says that in her past, she was strongly discouraged from being an active participant in sports, church, and social relationships:

*Girls sat and waited for the boy to act. Like we're property waiting to be bid on? Then we wait to be loved, kissed and then assaulted and raped!!! I think part of why I began TKD [Tae Kwon Do] was a small rebellious streak ... while TKD means much more to me than a rebellion against my upbringing, I do believe it was one bold way that I could make a statement about the kind of woman that I will be, and that woman wouldn't shy away from confrontation and could be empowered in a 'man's' world."* (Stambaugh)

This rebellious streak is best epitomized by Tae Yun Kim, the only woman to achieve grandmaster status in Tae Kwon Do. Grandmaster Kim had to overcome the challenges of being born female in a traditional male Korean household. When she was 8 years old, after seeing the male members of her household performing martial arts techniques, she convinced an old monk to begin teaching her Tae Kwon Do, even though this was forbidden. "Girls were expected to cook, get married and have 12 sons," she says. "But I didn't let that stop me. All my life, whenever anyone said, 'No, no, no!' I said, 'Yes, yes, yes!'" (Ransom, 65)

Grandmaster Kim came to the United States as a young adult, eventually becoming a chair of the Amateur Athletic Union and founding the first female Tae Kwon Do competition. She points out that martial arts help women in their daily lives, bringing "the balance needed to be a true champion in life. Through martial arts, you can conquer fear and self-doubt and take that confidence and put it to use in your personal life." (Ransom, 65) Kim goes on to say that women benefit when "they stop looking at clothes, looking at the external. Stop saying, 'I'm a girl...' say, 'I am me!' Other arenas in daily life discount girls' abilities, and in most cases girls don't even know what their own abilities are. They find out what they can do in martial arts. (*Ransom 65*)

Sometimes this rebellion takes a few years to manifest itself. A martial artist says she had always wanted to learn the sport but was not permitted to as a young girl. "But I had played organized sports since seventh grade. ... I had no more eligibility after college and the team thing got really old, and I wanted to do something for me. [In Tae Kwon Do] you motivate yourself." (Dumin). And you get to do something you have always wanted to do and defy the people who would not let you play when you were still a kid.

Other reasons for starting a contact sports are varied. One martial artist says she has "always been drawn to violent stuff— I enjoy guy movies not chick flicks," so the idea of playing a contact sport appealed to her even if the contact was intimidating at first. (Anderson, V.)

Sometimes proximity counts. A wrestling coach says he was first approached by girls who wanted to wrestle in 1980. A girl who was team manager at the time learned to wrestle informally. During practice, if there were an uneven number of boys, she'd pair up and wrestle. Other girls heard about this and signed on. Coach Anderson says invariably the girls who started wrestling had brothers or fathers who wrestled and this family background inspired them to learn how. (Anderson, B.) It also helped that they had the support of their families, since co-ed wrestling still holds the power to shock observers.

A hockey player explains that she became involved after reading articles in the newspaper about a women's hockey team in her city. "I had just started my first nursing job and had more time. I never knew anyone (male or female) who played hockey, but I thought that a group of women playing a traditionally male sport might be interesting women to know, so I tried and *loved it* (even though I was *really, really* terrible)." (Kangas, P.) She says that as a child she loved contact sports but could never play them on a team "or with any support from anywhere (tried to be on school teams and wasn't permitted because 'girls didn't play those sports')." She goes on to say that as a large, muscular woman, "it's appealing to see a sport where size isn't a hindrance." (Kangas, P.) It is clear that her motivating factor is not one single cause but a multitude of them. She was attracted to the idea of meeting the kind of people who would play a contact sport, she had been interested in contact sports previously but had been discouraged from them, so some small amount of rebellion probably entered into her decision, and her physical attributes made the sport a good fit for her. Although most women cite one or two main reasons why they were attracted to a contact sport, having a combination of several reasons is not uncommon.

Women report sitting on the sidelines watching others play as a common frustration. The cure? They take up the sport themselves. One athlete confirms this when she says she began playing hockey after she started dating a college hockey coach. "I knew that if I wanted to spend any time with him at all, I would have to learn [to play hockey]. Not a very politically correct reason, I suppose. But it worked for me. He has gone from my life, but hockey won't." (Wellman)

Another hockey player says, "My husband started playing roller hockey and ice hockey in 1996. It looked like a lot of fun, and I got kind of sick of sitting there in the cold watching him! He and his brother spent a lot of time encouraging me and scrounging up enough gear so that I could play." (Torrance) In the case of these two women, as in the case of many others like them, their boyfriends and husbands supported their decision to play a contact sport because it reinforced their own playing. It was something they could do together, or at least talk about together.

One hockey player, who learned the game from her brothers, even wrote an essay about the experience. (See Appendix, "Our Ice Rink" for full text.)

For others, it was watching their children play that finally motivated them to start:

*I had no sports background. I hated them. I was horrible at sports—avoided them at all costs. I had always wanted to try martial arts but I didn't want to go by myself and I couldn't get anyone to go with me. Then my daughter started taking classes and after a while I started too."* (Anderson, V.)

She explains that other parents with children had started taking classes and that motivated her. Her daughter only said, "Just don't embarrass me." (Anderson, V.)

One woman joined a martial arts school after watching her son participate for a time. The other members of the school encouraged her to start, and she decided that she needed the exercise and enjoyed the camaraderie. Although her son eventually quit the sport, she went on to earn her black belt. (Eaden) Another joined because she wanted her then-12-year-old daughter "to develop more confidence and assertiveness. Together we signed up for a six week beginner's course. ... Three and a half years later, I achieved my first degree black belt." Her daughter stopped taking lessons after earning her brown belt. (Robinson) What is interesting about almost all of these cases is that the women continued to play the sport long after their children had lost interest. Thus, although their children playing was a motivating factor—it got them started—it was not necessary for them to continue playing. Other factors, which will be discussed in the next chapter, create the conditions that make women reluctant to give up playing contact sports.

Others attribute "conspiracy" to their eventual involvement in contact sports. A rugby player says she was "set up" by her mother and a friend of her mother's:

*Brian* [a rugby player] *was single, too. ... We emailed back and forth, finally went out on a date and now are getting married. But back to the story. He suggested I come in and practice with the Barbarians* [a men's rugby team]. *I did. I used it to get in shape. ... It got to the point that I was making more of the practice than Brian was because of an injury. ... I finally decided, 'If I am practicing this hard and this much, then I want to play.' Playing in a real game with guys would be suicide* [so she found a women's league]. *... I was petrified. ... But there was something about that first tackle. I can't put my finger on it, but it is pure addiction.* (Park)

Other women played sports as children and either simply continued playing a beloved sport or eventually gravitated toward contact sports. The owner of the Women's Professional Football League's New England Storm always loved football as a child. The organization reports, "The vision probably began years ago when Melissa Korpasz first picked up a football and knew, as sure as she knew how to breathe, that she was meant to play the sport." ("Storm History")

A martial artist says:

*I started Arnis* [stick fighting] *when I was 8* [she is now in her early 20s] *at a summer program. My instructor encouraged my parents to allow me to continue training since*

*I took it so seriously. ... My dad always had me playing stuff. ... I play basketball and ski, ran track and cross country in school, and played softball."* (Anderson, C.)

She says the movie *Karate Kid* motivated her interest in martial arts but that the involvement of her family and friends (both of her parents are black belts) kept her focused on her goals. (Anderson, C.)

A rugby player says she had always played sports in her youth but:

*I didn't think I was good enough* [to make school teams]. *I figured I needed to find a team and a sport that was young where nobody knows too much. That way we're all starting at the same level. ... Also, it sounded 'tough.' Tackling, scrums, rucks, mauls, all with no protection except your mouthguard. Very hardcore.* (Womack)

One martial artist, who has been involved with various fitness activities and sports throughout her life, says:

*Although I became enamored with martial arts (thanks to the* Green Hornet *television show with Bruce Lee) at age 5, I was never able to undertake studies until I was 40. ... I had always been fairly athletic, but became bored ... with* [traditional] *fitness activities. I needed something a little more engaging, something that wouldn't seem such a 'waste of precious time.' I also was provided an epiphany when my boyfriend and I were mugged in our safe little neighborhood.* (Wensel)

Sometimes participating in a contact sports is a means for confronting the past. One woman says bluntly:

*I had an abusive background.* [I had an] *extreme need to be able to protect myself from harm. To be able to stand up and know that no one could ever hurt me again. ... I didn't want to hurt anyone, that's not my nature, I just didn't want anyone else to hurt me or my child.* (Troutwine)

34

A young single mother, she wanted to learn some self-defense skills and she had a friend whose husband was a black
belt in Tae Kwon Do and wanted to start a school. She, her
brother and sister all decided to join together, both to learn
self-defense skills and to support her friend's business venture.
"My motivators would be ... my friend needed students, my
desire to learn some self-defense, participation with my brother
and sister, and a flat out 'I'll show *you*' attitude." (Troutwine)

Another martial artist says, "I was never allowed to take gym
in school. [Starting Tang Soo Do] was probably partly escape,
partly a need for physical activity where I could prove I wasn't
helpless. ... I was most likely looking for a challenge." (Bunker)

Women from all backgrounds find that they can discover
their abilities when they participate in any contact sport. The
risk, the physical danger of a contact sport, reveals and builds
inner strength and courage, two elements that can profoundly
empower women.

In the martial arts, as in many contact sports, size is not an
issue. If you're a boxer or a wrestler, you are matched to those
in your weight class. You might need to bulk up or slim down
to fight at a certain weight if you're interested in title fights,
but the issue isn't whether you are attractive or not, and it's no
different from what male fighters are asked to do. Size is more
of an issue in hockey, rugby and football, but contrary to societal expectations, women in these contact sports do better if
they're bigger. "I have always thought I needed the right figure for sports," says one football player. "Absolutely wrong.
You just need the right sport for your figure." (Dutter). One
hockey player points out that her 5' 8" height and bigger than
average size made her "intimidating"—a good thing for a female forward on a co-ed hockey team.(Schimanski-Gross)

Involvement in sports makes women realize that size and
shape don't matter. Women who are fat can pick up the same

skills that women who are skinny pick up. Playing contact sports shows women that fitness can help them succeed in their sports goals, but that a narrow definition of femininity, such as is expressed in *Glamour* magazine, isn't very realistic or desirable.

Women are attracted to contact sports because they offer an alternative to traditional ideas of what is beautiful, what is fitting, what is appropriate for women to do.

## Chapter Three
# Why Women Stay Involved

During the Olympic trials for Tae Kwon Do in May 2000, the odds-on favorite to dominate the trials, Kay Poe, dislocated her knee during her semi-final match. She knew her quest for a berth on the Olympic team had ended. There was no way she could win the finals with a dislocated knee, so her Olympic career was over before it had even started.

Or maybe not. Her opponent in the finals was Esther Kim, her friend and training partner. Kim, who knew Poe was the superior athlete, bowed out of the match. Her forfeit allowed Poe to travel to Sydney to compete in the Olympics. "There are other ways to be a champion," Kim said at the time. Almost everyone in the martial arts community thought Kim had done the right and noble thing; others were less convinced. The *New York Times* even speculated that Kim forfeited because she didn't think she was good enough to compete in Sydney. ("Sydney: 20 to Watch")

It's hard to imagine a man in any sport forfeiting a chance to go to the Olympics. But for women in contact sports, it really isn't all about the winning. When you ask them why they remain in contact sports, even after injuries, even after they've grown older and less able to compete, women answer in a word: camaraderie. Where else can you find women (and men) who are an awful lot like you? Although people who play other sports—especially team sports—identify camaraderie as very important to them, it ranks especially high in contact sports, even individual contact sports such as Tae Kwon Do. In these sports, training partners and sparring partners are like teammates, although you may be competing against them.

Attempting to define why she plays a sport that is not only non-traditional for women, but also not very well known in the United States, Emily Carlson, a rugby player on the Kansas City Jazz, says:

*Not only do you develop bonds like you do in any team experience, but the difference with rugby is you can go anywhere in the world and you have friends automatically. ... That's something you don't find in other sports. Rugby is a game of camaraderie. You can be out on the field in a knockdown, drag-out fight and as soon as the game is over, everyone's friends. That's what I like.* (Covitz)

Another rugby player says, "My best friends are all old rugby teammates." (Keyt) A martial artist says much the same thing: "I had a lot more in common with my Tae Kwon Do friends than my school mates. For one thing, they were more mature." (Anderson, C.) When asked why she stays involved in the sport, another martial artist says succinctly: "Community." (Robinson)

Carol Stambaugh, a black belt martial artist who has started her own self-defense consulting company, says there are many different reasons she stuck with the sport, camaraderie being only one of them:

*For a long time it was the socialization with a great group of friends. Another reason is health benefits. When I hurt my knee several years ago, I stopped working out for a good nine months. The increase in my migraine headaches had a direct correlation with me not working out. Being married to a black belt* [her husband has black belts in karate and Tae Kwon Do] *has helped keep me active and focused as well, because we do it together. ... [My instructors] have a lot to offer. ... they respect what we have to offer. ... The reasons for involvement now are much more personal and internal. After eleven years I still have goals to achieve and ways to get better. ... At the core, quitting TKD simply was not an option.* (Stambaugh)

This description of how women's reasons for involvement change over time is apt. Many women in contact sports report similar experiences. One rugby player says, "At first, I enjoyed learning not to be afraid of my body. Later, I enjoyed the feeling of playing. [Rugby] opened the door to other physical activities. ... Now I'm always showing off my bruises and saying, 'Look at the cleat marks!'" (Uzelac)

Another rugby player agrees that there are many reasons she stays involved and that her reasons for staying in the sport have evolved over time:

*I stay involved in the sport for so many reasons! I love playing on a team. With each game, you learn something new and you learn something about yourself. Rugby keeps me active while encouraging me to push myself. It also has improved my self-confidence and self-esteem. I love the contact, I love tackling, mauling, rucking. ... I love using my strength and strategies to improve my game. ... I have met amazing people through rugby. ... I love the game and I love the people who play the game. Rugby empowered me.* (Fancy)

This rugby player also says, "The great thing about rugby is there is truly a place for everyone. It doesn't matter how big or small you are. There is a position." (Fancy)

A hockey player agrees that finding her niche was essential to her continued involvement in contact sports:

*I started as a forward, did OK but never felt comfortable. Then I got switched to defense but still didn't feel quite right. Then the goalie ... developed some knee problems and we needed a backup, so I volunteered (thinking I'd better like this since the next stop is goal judge). And there I have stayed for 11 years ... I love hockey for its speed, excitement, and pure enjoyment ... I've made a lot of great friends playing the sport (my husband, my matron-of-honor, and half our wedding party).* (Formosa)

Others explain that the physical contact is the most important element, the one thing that keeps them coming back. One hockey player says, "I enjoy hitting people. Especially men. They get this look of surprise when they look up and realize they've gotten nailed by a girl." (Lentz) Another hockey player agrees: "I like the toughness of hockey (not the fighting but some pushing and shoving is fun)." (Torrance)

A rugby player calls the playing field a "battleground." (Keyt) One rugby player emailed me a list of rugby bumper stickers she thinks capture the spirit of rugby (Womack):

*Rugby/Elegant Violence*

*Give Blood/Play Rugby*

*Football Is For People Who Can't Play Rugby*

*Yes, Mom, I Still Play Rugby*

A member of the Vienna Mermaids tackle football team relates a portion of the team's training cadence to demonstrate the team's toughness (and possibly their sense of humor):

*Mermaids' defense sticks like glue*

*Is gonna beat the s\*\*\* out of you*

*Mermaids' offense just kicks ass*

*Is gonna dig your face into grass*

Another rugby player says, "It's a very primal sport in my opinion. You use brute force to push your opponents out of your way. You combine your force with your teammates to hit the opposing team. I think it's the feeling of power that keeps me coming back." (Womack)

One martial artist says, simply: "I learned I loved to fight." (Troutwine)

The feeling of toughness is essential to many women's participation in contact sports. The physical contact and risk are perceived as exhilarating and liberating. "People assume women take martial arts for self-defense," one martial arts instructor says. "Or because it's something active and better than aerobics. They don't understand how much we enjoy the physical contact." (Anderson, V.)

Others acknowledge that toughness is important but that there are other reasons they enjoy playing contact sports. A former equestrienne-turned-football-player says she was looking for "a cheap way to get the adrenaline, risk, bruises and fun" she used to experience as a rider. (Poehler) "The camaraderie is important," she says, but she also enjoys "getting outside to play a sport. I don't miss a practice. I don't miss a game." This basic enjoyment is echoed by another football player who says, "I like being out there running around, letting out my aggression, learning strategies and plays." (Noah)

Playing a contact sport requires building reserves of energy and determination. Many women relish those feelings as well. A boxer says, "You're working to get more and more power physically. ... You may have four rounds to go and you can't just break down and leave the ring." (McCaughey, 93) Many women echo this feeling of appreciating being forced to "dig deep" and discover their inner resources. Another boxer says, "There's something about boxing that's so raw and so emotional. ... And you can't escape if you're in the ring. You're already committed, you're already in there. So it forces you to confront things you might be able to avoid otherwise." (McCaughey, 114)

Some women simply embrace the sport without questioning their specific reasons for involvement. One hockey player has this to say:

> *I stay involved with hockey for only one reason—I love playing the game. ... While I was pregnant, I coached instead of playing and thought that after I had my daughter I would cut back on playing and do more coaching. But less than two weeks after she was born, I was right back out playing. ... I couldn't give up playing so I gave up coaching.* (Hallada-Pinhey)

Others find it difficult to precisely articulate what about their experience keeps them coming back. What they do know, however, is that playing a contact sport becomes tied to their self-image. "I absolutely loved my training," says a martial artist. "I had what I considered to be the very best teachers. The senior ... students were overwhelmingly supportive. Even though I had a great deal of confidence in myself, my sense of purpose became somehow more defined while training. Training and achieving my black belt was, in a nutshell, empowering." (Robinson) Many women share this belief that participating in contact sports helps define and refine a woman's essence. One player says:

> *Rugby defines part of who I am. It's something I love to do. I love the moment in the scrum, when everyone is bound together, waiting, anticipating, looking down and seeing a grasshopper land on someone's shoelaces, and thinking how peaceful things are right before the moment of impact.* (Womack)

She goes on to explain how she enjoys the physical release:

> *I love feeling my muscles stretch and work to their full capacity. I love the complete, whole body tiredness after a game, feeling that I am completely spent. I like how people look at me when I tell them I play. It's a point of pride for me.* (Womack)

Another rugby player says her participation helped her overcome an eating disorder and helped her "stop apologizing for the space I take up in the world." (Keyt)

Several martial artists have agreed that martial arts training (and training in other contact sports) transforms participants. One coach said, "They move on; they end unhealthy relationships; they quit their jobs; they go back to school. They jump out of planes! They climb mountains; they start new business ... they unleash that chain." (McCaughey, 122) Other coaches and participants point out that women in contact sports stand up for themselves more, both in their personal lives and in their work lives.

The transformative effects of contact sports is a powerful motivator for women to continue their participation. A martial artist says, "People still find it hard to believe I could do anything like that. I'm still only 5' 4" and weigh around 125, still feminine, but I'm a very strong person, inside I mean. People know me as a risk taker, a person who's not afraid to try anything." (Troutwine) Before, she says, she was shy and introverted, unwilling to try anything new.

Contact sports allow women to define their lives. They decide what they are going to do with their bodies. When they play football or rugby or hockey, they're no longer someone's daughter or mother or girlfriend. Opponents and spectators have to respect them as individuals in one capacity: athlete. Their social identity and their personal identity may become inextricably bound up with their athleticism, their participation in sports. Female athletes, sports historian Lissa Smith says, "repossess their bodies." (x) Women who participate in contact sports agree, saying over and over that it gives them something that cannot be taken away. Sports historian Susan K. Cahn says this is not unusual: "The satisfaction of sport [becomes] a crucial part of identities forged in rebellion against restrictive gender conventions." (235) Women who are non-conformists, who are rebellious, tend to find the contact sports appealing. "Yeah, I'm a wife and a mother," they say. "And I can still kick your ass."

A person in rebellion often feels the need to show "them"—outsiders, naysayers—what she can do. A feeling of rebellion, of defiance, motivates many people to start playing a contact sport. It also motivates many women to *continue* playing a contact sport. One martial artist explains, "I had something big to prove to my family ... that I could succeed where they thought I would fail" (Bunker). Another agrees with this assessment: "My father was a factor ... (but not in a positive way). ... He used to say, 'What position do you play? The bench?' Because of my father," she says simply, "I felt that I had to be good at whatever I do." (Grabowski) Women who compete in sports, especially contact sports, report over and over that while they may have defied society, more personally, they have defied their fathers.

Sports historian Smith says, "Athletic training implicitly challenges patriarchal constraints on a woman's behavior." (xii) In many women's lives, this challenge is not abstract or implied, it is concrete. The patriarch in question is called Dad.

Women in contact sports not only "repossess their bodies," they gain confidence in their ability to withstand potential violence. A boxer says, "It's good to be able to take a punch. We think we'll be overwhelmed, but we can handle it." (McCaughey, 93) Another boxer echoes this sentiment: "There [is] a kind of power in being actually able to take a punch ... and even being able to give it, [give] a really good strong punch." She goes on to say, "Maybe you could take the punch [from an attacker] and still fight, even if it did daze you." (McCaughey, 106) The more they participate in contact sports, the less they feel frightened by physical violence. Letting go of that fear, which keeps many woman contained, constrained, and hidden away, is a powerful factor in continuing participation in contact sports.

A martial artist who has trained since childhood says that when she was a teenager, parents always asked their daughters if she was going along when they went out at night. It was always assumed that she could take care of her friends, that she could protect them. "I kind of think it's cool that they [the parents] had that confidence in me," she says. (Anderson, C.)

In fact, this confidence translates into freedom. "Empowering" is a word that gets used a lot. So is "liberating." For these women, empowerment is not an abstract ideal.

"I didn't know what [rugby] was," says one player of her first session on the field. But the sensation and intensity of playing she found "liberating." She goes on to explain: "We could beat the hell out of each other during a game, then have a party afterwards." (Keyt)

"I love the camaraderie," says a hockey player "[and] the physical nature of the sport. It's not that I'm a bruiser, but when you get into the game, it's fun to be able to push people around. ... It takes a lot of thought and skill to play the game well, so it's mentally stimulating as well." (Waddell-Rutter)

The power women feel—the power they *earn*—derives from the physicality of the sport. They believe there is a strong connection between the physical contact and the exhilaration they feel. Playing a non-contact sport would never affect them in the same way.

"I like the aggression of the sport," says Celeste Daughenbaugh, a rugby player who is a scientist by day. "I like the power." (Covitz)

A hockey player says:

*I think it's almost to prove to myself that I can do it. That I can stick up to guys who play out there, that although I'm smaller and perhaps a bit slower, I can still hang and be an asset to the team. Another reason I stay is the way it makes me feel. There's nothing like slipping the puck in the net around the goalie and watching your team, the crowd, your coaches, cheer for you. There's nothing like the teamwork it takes to win a game and the leadership it can bring out in a person.* (Wellman)

She goes on to relate the story of a memorable game that, even though a loss, made her feel great. "Nobody could take me down and no one could get near me. ... I have never felt better about myself on the ice than that night. I knew I was a contender and a physical presence on the ice. That made me a success in my mind." (Wellman)

The women in contact sports also recognize that their peers enjoy the feelings of toughness, of physical contact associated with violent sports. A martial artist-turned-rugby player says:

*I met a lot of women who thought themselves very tough and who didn't shy away from being hurt. It was like a big circle of comrades-in-arms, suffering together and then celebrating the mere aspect of surviving the ordeal. It made me feel good to work that hard, to take the hits, to go home battered (much like the martial arts) and to have trophies of my toughness ... my bruises.* (Bunker)

A boxing instructor points out that while women start boxing for various reasons, it is always the sparring that keeps them coming back. This is often true of women who participate in martial arts as well. Although sparring is at first frightening—even, some say, traumatic—it is that very aspect of training that attracts so many women and propels them to continue participating in the sport. Martial arts scholar and feminist Martha McCaughey comments that "the pleasurable character of combative bodily practices no doubt reflects the pleasurable character of becoming a new kind of woman" (114).

This new woman is tough, confident and not afraid of violence. Over and over, women emphasize their love of the contact in contact sports.

A rugby-turned-football player says, "When changing from [playing] rubgy to football, my fear was that there wasn't enough contact, but alas, there is plenty!" (Walker)

Jessica Howard, an offensive lineman for a high school football team, says, "[Getting hit] is what I love about the game. It's physical. Sometimes you hit them and sometimes they hit you. It's fun"(Carter). Her mother, Julie Howard, thought Jessica would drop football when she got to middle school, but she didn't. "It's to the point now where it's really not that big of a deal. She's been playing with these boys since the sixth grade and she's just one of the guys," the elder Howard says. A classmate, Jacob Grey, says, "It think it's cool. Everyone just kind of thinks that. If she's good and can go out there and compete with the guys, why shouldn't she play?" (Carter)

At the same time, some participants insist that the contact part of contact sports is not their primary motivation for continuing the sport. One hockey player points out, "Hockey is as much a mental game as it is a physical." (Ward) A boxer says, "It's cerebral. ... It's not about hitting them as hard as you can or trying to take them out. ... It's about trying to outdo them, being a smart fighter." (McCaughey, 108) A football player says, "Some women are basically there to knock heads and show off their brute strength, but 9 out of 10 times you can beat them with talent." (Walsh)

A hockey player says, "It's a mental challenge. I like playing for teams that need me to play really well in order for everyone to succeed. I like coming through for the team." (Torrance) Another hockey player says, "It combines exercise and camaraderie ... teamwork, contact, finesse. There is *always* more to learn. When I am on the ice, there is nothing else. No bills, no kids, no job, no boss; just the puck, the ice, the team, the opponent. ... Life is very simple." (Kangas, P.) Many women point out that contact sports allow for pr    ecious moments of transcedence that occur when all of one's mind and energy are focused on a physical task.

A rugby player says:

*It is an addiction of sorts. Not an obsession. Not a control thing, but a rejuvenation. ... It can be grueling but never unfulfilling. ... I am a self-employed, successful Realtor, on my way to higher and higher goals. I work hard, often under very high stress for deadlines and negotiating and it is mentally draining. A rough and physically taxing sport to me is the only 'balance' for that kind of mental drain.* (Park)

A rubgy player says, "[I] had little time for social/leisure activity. Therefore, practice time was always 'me time.' I could be working on a huge project, stressed out of my mind, but when I played rugby, I forgot everything else. Tackling and hitting (with body, not fist) were wonderful stress relievers." (Womack)

A hockey player agrees that "it's a great stress reliever" but she finds more satisfaction in helping others learn the game, helping them become better people and better players:

*I want to do all I can to make sure the game is just as fun for them as it was and is for me. I love to see more and more girls and women in hockey because it's typically been a male sport. I love to see the girls stick up for themselvees and say, "Hey, I love the game, and I'm going to play."* (Kangas, G.)

Others agree that there are many intrinsic rewards to the sport, not all having to do with contact. A martial artist explains, "I became extremely attracted to physical fitness. The more I worked out ... the better I felt. My mind and spirit reached a whole new level. I was closer to God and more thankful than ever for my existence." (Troutwine) Another martial artist explains how rewarding her experience has been: "The friendships and self-esteem [are] uncommonly satisfying." With some encouragement from her instructors, she began competing in tournaments. "I took a silver medal in the fighting competition and was named a member of the United States Kali Team 2000. Other than the births of my two sons, it was the most exciting and fulfilling experience of my life." (Wensel)

A hockey player tells a story that she feels sums it up:

*Every year in the men's league a story circulates about a guy who comes in the first day of the season and says, "You won't see me again because this is just a cover—I'm having an affair while my wife thinks I'm playing hockey." Someone told this story in a women's locker room and there was dead silence, then someone spoke what we all were thinking: "Why would you have an affair when you could be playing hockey?"* (Kangas, P.)

Women participate in contact sports for many reasons. They say it develops stamina, strength and mental toughness, making things women go through, like childbirth, easy—or easier. They say they love the feeling of toughness they get from playing a contact sport. The contact makes them more able to handle the emotional and physical challenges life dishes out. For some, it helps them come to terms with past violence and abuse— here, they are in control, and they can dish it out, too. The relationships they make participating in contact sports— whether the sport is an individual sport or a team sport—encourage them to continue their participation. And even after retiring from professional or amateur careers, many stay involved in the sport recreationally, for fun. Many coach, or, like me, write books about their sport.

One thing's for sure: women don't do it for the money. Professional women boxers make about $200 a round. The few women martial artists who try to make a living at it can't; they work as bodyguards, stunt doubles and consultants. Although some women in contact sports can play at the college level for scholarship money, there isn't a professional league that pays a living wage. But that doesn't stop women from playing contact sports and from excelling at them.

Maybe they like the camaraderie, or the role models they meet, or the idea that life can be lived in a different way. But they are absolutely intolerant of women who don't play hard. One martial artist says, "in training ... some women cry and act so soft, I hate it! Be tough and achieve!" (Robinson) She echoes words that most women in contact sports believe. One fighter says, "This is not for everyone. This is not ballet." (Stambaugh) If you're going to cry and act soft, play another game. Not a contact sport. The women who play contact sports seriously feel they have to make a distinction between themselves and the women who don't play hard. Their intolerance stems from their belief that expressing weakness or pain reflects badly on all women and sets back the "cause" of women in contact sports. They feel that perception is important, and it important that others—men, outsiders—understand that the women who play contact sports don't want special consideration or to be treated any differently from the men who play contact sports.

What they like is this strange illusion they have, this belief they cherish, that on the field or in the training hall, there is no gender, there is no masculine, no feminine; it's irrelevant. There's no class, no race; it doesn't matter. What one does off the field or outside the training hall is completely removed from what one does inside.

The outside world doesn't seem much interested in women in contact sports. In sports journalism, something like 95% of all reporting is about men. Only by staying involved in sports can women see the changes that are being made. When the only women who are featured in *Sports Illustrated* are in the swimsuit edition, it can be discouraging. But that's why women keep going back to training. Otherwise, where are they going to find their good female role models? Certainly not in other magazines about women's sports—*Sports Illustrated for Women* might have articles about sporting events, but sadly these are overwhelmed by the number of articles on how to have shiny hair after a workout. The concentration is still on "Swim Yourself Thin!" (Headline from cover of *Women's Sports and Fitness*, July/August 2000).

The majority of women see their actual participation in contact sports limited by age or injury but expect to continue their involvement as spectators, coaches, officials, leaders. Many of the women who have children involve their children in their sport (or at least in other sports). Most want to be good role models for their children. A martial artist says, "My daughter was always very proud of me. ... She speaks of my martial arts with pride, that her 'little' Mom could do such a thing" (Troutwine). One hockey player says, "My son, who is 9, has played hockey since he was 5. I started playing at that time as well because I wanted someone to skate with him and having grown up in Canada, I knew the game well." Her daughter, now 5, also skates. She says her son is especially proud that she is an assistant coach on his travel team and asks questions like, "Mommy, how come there are no other moms coaching teams we play?" She says, "I started to play hockey ... so that I could share a sport that I knew my children would love and play one day." (Wiechers)

Another hockey player says

*My daughter ... has no idea that hockey is considered by many to be a "men's" sport. She has probably seen more women and girls playing than men ... [my] two older neph-*

*ews ... have been heard bragging about their aunt's hockey ability. ... The older one, especially, is very respectful of girls and women playing at a high level with boys/men.* (Hallada-Pinhey)

A martial artist whose daughter is also in the sport says, "She thought it was cool and helped me all the time. She demanded more from me than the adult coaches did." (Anderson, V.) A football player relates how a teammate's son comes to all the games to hold the down markers and to cheer on his mother. (Poehler) A martial artist explains that there are many mothers at her school, and they train together with their children. Outsiders occasionally criticize this practice as teaching children to be violent, although most martial artists maintain that children involved in the martial arts are less violent and aggressive than those who aren't. (Dumin)

Some women go through extraordinary struggles to stay involved in contact sports even during difficult times of their lives. One martial artist credits her involvement in Tae Kwon Do with helping her stay physically and emotionally fit while being treated for breast cancer. Others have continued playing through job losses, cross-country moves, divorces and the deaths of loved ones. A hockey player says:

*Hockey is the greatest game I've ever played. As well as all the friends that I have made playing this game, it has been a welcomed distraction for me as I have battled cancer and other challenges I have faced throughout the years. My coaches have carefully placed garbage cans on the bench in case I am sick between shifts at a game following chemo-therapy, and I've rarely missed a game or practice because of my illness. Indeed, I am told by health care workers that the passion I have for everything I do in life has definitely played a huge role in my survival and my tolerance of treatments* (Wiechers).

The reasons why women stay involved in contact sports, despite the disapproval of friends and family, despite injuries they may receive, may change over time, but are related to the reasons they started participating in a contact sport—camaraderie, feelings of worth, of power and strength, the sense of liberation and autonomy that comes with participating in a non-traditional sport.

## Chapter Four
# What Kind of Women Are They?

They have big butts. And small ones. And all in-between sizes. There's no one particular kind of person, no special kind of woman, who participates in violent sports.

Observers often assume that women who get involved in contact sports are making a statement. Many of them, indeed, consider themselves feminists, although they may shy away from using the term. Many, however, do not consider themselves feminists by any stretch of the imagination. Christy Martin, the first female professional boxer to become famous (as indicated by the fact that she signed with Don King, the notorious promoter who doesn't sign anyone who's not capable of turning a profit), swears she's not a feminist and says, "I'm not out to make a statement about women in boxing or even women in sports." (Sekules 19) Billing herself as "The Coal Miner's Daughter," Martin has also said she would never want a daughter of hers involved in boxing. Women like Martin simply see themselves as exceptions to the rules, doing what they want to do and not necessarily expecting other women to follow suit—or to want to follow suit. They don't think of themselves as trailblazers or as women making a statement about what women can do. Instead, they are simply doing what feels right for them.

This does not mean that outsiders don't have other, sometimes harmful, perceptions of them. Historically, women have been considered masculine or mannish if they participate in sport. Those who participate in contact sports are especially vulnerable to this stereotyping. For this reason, women athletes sometimes overemphasize their femininity. The athlete as beauty queen has a lengthy past (Cahn 78) and even this year's crop of homecoming queens counts a couple of football linebackers among them. Female athletes sometimes see this balancing of the obviously feminine with the historically masculine as a form of success. "This Homecoming Princess Has Game on the Football Field" is the title of a recent newspaper article. It is not the only one of its kind.

Sociologists call this the "feminine apologetic": the idea that we have to make female athletes appealing to men in order for them to be acceptable. (Theberge 160) Participating in sports, especially contact sports, might make one seem masculine, which makes one unattractive to men, non-marriageable. Many women refuse to challenge this proposition, feeling it is only natural for a heterosexual woman to want to attract heterosexual men. Instead of challenging the perception that it is not "feminine" to participate in sports, they acommodate by dressing sexy, wearing makeup, and talking about men. (Dowling, 24)

Sportswriter Mariah Burton Nelson says, "this sexualization of sports is disturbing for many reasons, primarily because women use sports as a way to become appealing to men rather than a way to discover their own power." (106)

Olympic athlete Anna Seaton Huntington believes that many people are ambivalent about aggressive women and "may initially balk at the knowledge that most female athletes don't care what they look like, sound like or smell like as long as they are crossing the finish line first." (Zimmerman, 9) This counters, even threatens, our concept of what is feminine, what is womanly, so it isn't uncommon for an athlete to don high heels as soon as she wins the competition, to "prove" that she is still feminine, still in all important respects a woman.

Sports historian Allen Guttmann says, "aggressiveness ... has conventionally been more closely associated with men than with women. It follows, therefore, that a commitment to women's sports has almost always been to some degree problematical—in women's eyes as well as men's." (3)

This preoccupation with the femininity or lack thereof of women in contact sports was evidenced in my own experience when a (male) judge presiding over a promotion test looked out over the students lined up in front of him and said, "There are some pretty women in this group." As if that mattered to us, as if we needed to have our beauty acknowledged, as if we hadn't just grunted and sweated for 45 minutes trying to show our strength, focus, determination and resolve. In one stroke, he put us in our place: we were still women—lesser than men—but at least we were pretty.

Some of the women in contact sports express an eagerness to destroy standard notions of femininity. One rugby player characterizes soccer and other popular women's sports this way: "You can wear ponytails and look pretty." (Keyt) It is obvious that this does not appeal to her. A martial artist says, "Everyone dresses the same—in uniforms that resemble pajamas. You don't have to look cute." (Anderson, V.) A hockey coach, discussing her choice of sport, says, "I just wasn't a ponytailed ... kind of girl." (McDowell) The ponytailed female athlete stands as a symbol for these women—the type of athlete who must assert her femininity while playing. Long hair stands for attractiveness to men. Short hair, much more practical for athletes, is perceived as mannish. These women dispute the idea that they're mannish or that they're trying to be like men. It isn't about gender, or some fragile definition of masculine or feminine; it is about being whole individuals who understand what they and their bodies can do. One martial artist sums it up: "I've been on my own a lot of years and have always done the 'man' things as well as the 'woman' things." (Troutwine) A hockey player says she has "a history of jobs in male-dominated fields (factory, security guard, wastewater plant)." (Kangas, P.)

"Nice girls don't do things like this," says one rugby player, summing up the difference between women who play traditional women's sports and women who play contact sports. (Uzelac)

Because the masculinity associated with athletic performance (especially in contact sports) calls into question the femininity of female athletes, their sexual orientation becomes suspect. Allegations and perceptions of rampant lesbianism affect all women in sports. It is still quite common for outsiders to assume that women in sports, especially women in contact sports, must be lesbians.

One martial artist points out that people assume that because she participates in a violent sport, she must be a lesbian. Or else "desperate to meet guys or something stupid like that." (Eaden) A boxer says, "I hesitate telling people that I box ... because I'm afraid I'll be labeled a lesbian. It already happened to me. And I have nothing against gays; it's just that I am not gay and I'm afraid I'll get ... labeled a lesbian and then men will dislike me." This anxiety about labels is most pronounced in young adult women. Women in their later 20s and 30s express fewer concerns about this, possibly because heterosexual women have often married and/or started families by then. They may also be more comfortable with themselves and less concerned about the perceptions of others.

The charge of lesbianism is a particularly common one, report most of the single women I interviewed, as if participating in sports can somehow turn an otherwise heterosexual woman into a flaming lesbian. Of course, several of the women pointed out that in their cases it was true, they are lesbians and are certainly not ashamed of it. The preoccupation with women's sexual orientation, so irrelevant to sport, appears to be one way society forces women to conform to more conventional gender roles. The message is clear: If you don't want to be considered a lesbian, don't act like one.

Because women in sports, especially contact sports, seem unconcerned with appropriate gender behavior, labeling them as lesbians serves to underscore an important point: lesbian women are not under the control of men. This threatens the very fabric of patriarchal society, much as women participating in contact sports threatens male notions of physical and athletic superiority. Historian Susan K. Cahn points out, "the fear of female sexuality unleashed from feminine modesty and male control runs like a constant thread through the history of women's sport." (163) By the late 1950s, she says, all female athletes, physical education teachers and coaches "operated under a cloud of sexual suspicion." (Cahn, 181) They continue to do so to the present time.

At the same time, the charges of lesbianism are often true. While 10% of the general population is thought to be gay, there is a higher proportion of lesbians in sports, including contact sports. It is possible that heterosexual women are more susceptible to constraints on their behavior and settle for more "feminine" outlets. Sportswriter Mariah Burton Nelson also speculates that if a lesbian competes with men or boys and they disapprove, the disapproval is much less meaningful to her than it is to a heterosexual women. She says, "Sports do not create lesbians ... but they may, like other liberating experiences, create opportunities." (148)

A football player points out that one of the attractions of the sport to her is its strong lesbian community of players and supporters. (Noah) One rugby player says:

> *For several seasons when I played rugby, I was the only straight woman on the team. ... It may be a self-perpetuating prophecy. Meaning, the stereotype is that lesbians are in sports, therefore, the gay community moves towards the sporting circles to meet others. ... I do not know many women who are not afraid to take a hit or get a bruise or break a nail. They called us tomboys when we were younger and I think to some extent we were teased then and started to try to be more conventional growing up.* (Park)

She speculates that women playing contact sports tend to be those willing to defy gender conventions. Several of the women openly spoke about their lesbianism and tended to agree that their identification as lesbians made them more willing to defy convention and to ignore pressure or disapproval from others about their participation in contact sports.

One sports psychologist reports that he receives more questions about the dangers of sports to girls' sexuality (ie, the "danger" of becoming a lesbian) than any other topic. (Nelson 142) Contact sports and traditionally male sports are always rumored to be full of lesbians. (Nelson 144) It seems to be an abiding obsession among observers.

Especially in professional sports, many lesbians try to "pass." Otherwise, paychecks and corporate sponsorships can be threatened. Sportswriter Nelson says lesbian women "passing" for heterosexual "exacerbates the homophobia of the men who own, organize, finance and control women's sports." (134) The only way to reduce this homophobia, she feels, is for women to acknowledge their sexual orientation.

In the end, whether one is a lesbian or not, and how one feels about lesbianism is irrelevant: the point is that participating in sports is viewed as unnatural for woman and therefore the woman who plays a sport (especially a contact sport) must be "unnatural" in other ways. To avoid being lumped into a category that she may find threatening or uncomfortable, female participants in sports find the display of outward signs of femininity to be very important.

Often women become less concerned about these outward signs of femininity and the perceptions of outsiders the longer they play. The women I interviewed who play in a certain amount of anonymity (ie, those who play in recreational leagues) find this easier to do. Female athletes who are constantly in the spotlight tend to be more concerned about appearance and perception. Given the unrelenting pressure of the media, this preoccuppation with appearances is certainly understandable, however regrettable it may be.

While some women who play contact sports are most assuredly lesbians, many also live ordinary lives as wives and mothers (and some of the lesbians also live ordinary lives as mothers). Manon Rheume, the first woman to play professional ice hockey, first in an exhibition game in the NHL, then more regularly in the IHL, became a mother in 1999, and still planned to compete in the 2002 Olympic Games. Editors called this story "Mama Manon: Motherhood doesn't diminish Rheaume's pipe dreams," although why her dreams are "pipe dreams" isn't clear. She's perfectly capable of playing her sport even after childbirth, a fact that seems elusive to the male sportswriters who report on women in sports.

About one-third of the women I interviewed said they were lesbians, approximately three times as many as one might expect to find in the general population. Of the remaining, about one third are married and have children; an additional 10% - 15% are married but childless. Some of the single and divorced women and a few of the lesbians have children, as well. The rest are single women with no children. However, I do not pretend that the numbers presented here represent anything but the women who answered my request for interviews. The results are not reliable for statistical purposes since the interviewees were self-selected, and many knew one another; there was no attempt to randomly identify and interview women in contact sports. Indeed, I depended on the interviewees to put me in contact with other women who played contact sports. It is not my contention that this was a scientifically conducted survey that will yield reproducible results. I was merely interested in talking to some women about their experiences in contact sports, and I was fortunate to find a wonderful group of eloquent, intelligent and interesting women on the first try.

None of the mothers I spoke to let having children get in the way of participating in contact sports. Most played at least part of the time they were pregnant and most were back to full participation within a month or two after the birth of their children. One hockey player who discovered she was pregnant early in her ice hockey days says, "I played until my parents were able to come to a game. ... Then I became a cheering section and videographer." Two months after her daughter was born, she began competing again:

> *I nursed her, so I brought her to most of the away games. ... I would nurse her in the locker room. It kinda surprised one ref when he came in to clarify some scoring. ... Erin* [her daughter] *did not always enjoy the night games but she loved it when we won the Ruicci cup in the afternoon. I got a lot of praise when I walked into the rink with her in a back carrier, my equipment bag over one shoulder and my sticks and diaper bag on the other.* (Schimanski-Gross)

She says, further, "I want to show [my daughters] healthy habits. I'm making time in my life for physical activity; so should they . ... They think only women play hockey. I don't want anyone telling them 'you can't do that because you're a girl.'"

Another hockey player, who is married to a hockey player and who has four hockey-playing children, says, "We are hockey poor. We live in a teeny house and drive crummy cars so we can all play hockey. It's a highly addictive sport. Almost no one plays 'a little.'" She says her daughter especially likes it "because we both play and we can play together, and I understand her passion." She relates a story that sums up her family's feelings about her involvement:

*I did a clinic with teenage boys. My husband said, "Well, I bet they think it's cool that you're out there." I replied, "No, they think I'm old and slow and in their way." My 11-year-old boy chipped in, "Yeah, but I bet you're better than their moms!" I loved him for that! (Kangas, P.).*

Most of the women in contact sports feel committed to the sport, a commitment that lasts a lifetime. Although not all women in contact sports have been sports-oriented all their lives (I for one came to it relatively late in life), often the women who end up playing contact sports have played many different sports throughout their lives, and this is just one more way of exploring their abilities, their physicality. Many have been athletic all their lives, with parents and siblings who participated in sports.

One martial artist echoes the comments of many women in contact sports when she says, "I have always been what was called a tomboy. Dolls and dressing up were not my cup of tea. Especially when there were boys outside who needed players for football or just playing chase. Being fairly athletic and having some success with organized sports was to me the best part of school." (Robinson)

A hockey player says, "I was always a jock. None of my three brothers lettered in high school, but I did. I always played boys' games. I was never excluded." (Lentz)

"I guess I've always been somewhat of a tomboy," says a rugby player. "I've always had the desire to prove myself, to prove my strength. Rugby became my proof." (Fancy)

"I've always been a bit of a tomboy and a rough and tumble kind of girl," summarizes a hockey player. (Waddell-Rutter)

Women recount stories of playing with boys throughout their youth, then entering a period of being relegated to girls' teams or girls' sports, then deciding that they missed the physical contact of the sports they played when young and seeking to rediscover that feeling of exhilaration through contact sports.

"I used to play on the backyard rink with my four older brothers," says one hockey player who took up ice hockey in her 30s, many years after she had given it up. "I last skated when I was about 15 or 16—I had not had a stick in hand since our last backyard ice rink during the blizzard of '78." She says:

*Figure skating wasn't for me, and my dad filed the spikes off my figure skates to make it easier for me to do a hockey stop. ... I loved to play and played any position my brothers told me, just so I could play with them in the backyard... In sixth grade I had to write an essay on the subject of what I would accomplish 20 years later. I wrote that I would become a professional hockey player. ... That is the last time I remember thinking I could and would be a hockey player... [My mother] did not want me to play on a boys' team and there were not enough girls who signed up to make a team... I became a fan rather than a player.* (Schimanski-Gross)

She concludes rather wistfully, "I know I'm never going to be in the Olympics, but I'm going to do this as long as I can," echoing the sentiments of many women who, in the words of sportswriter Mariah Burton Nelson, are in "mourning for something that never had a chance to develop its potential." (34)

But like many women, Schimanski-Gross rediscovered her first love as an adult and plays enthusiastically at the recreational level. She says, "This past year, when my husband searched for a new job, I told him I would go anywhere, as long as I could continue to play women's hockey. I had waited until age 31 to play and I was not about to give it up—I want to play for the rest of my life." (Schimanksi-Gross)

For those women who came to sports later in life, contact sports reveal, often for the first time, what they and their bodies can do. These women may have arrived at sports after everyone else has, but they become as committed to them as women who have played sports since the time they could walk. One such woman says, "I was not athletic. But training in the martial arts was like learning a powerful dance. My body could do things I never believed possible." (Friesen)

Although women in contact sports share certain general traits—an admiration for toughness, an impatience with traditional ideas of what women can do, one thing has become clear: there isn't a typical woman who participates in contact sports. Just as the reasons for joining a violent sport vary from person to person, the type of person who participates also varies. They are social workers, music teachers and stay-at-home moms. They are reporters, nurses and scientists. They are African-American, Chicana, Asian and white. They are Christians and Jews and atheists. Some are loud and boisterous; some are shy and soft-spoken; some are wives and mothers, some are childfree, some have partners of the same sex, or of both sexes depending on the day. Some are feminists, some are not. Some see their participation in the context of larger women's issues, others do not. Some have played sports all their lives, others are new to the experience. All of them, however, are quite positive that playing contact sports changed their lives—for the better.

## Chapter Five
# Men Versus Women

Half of all females registered with USA Hockey play on boys' or men's teams, even though there are more than one thousand girls' and women's teams scattered across the United States. Why do women insist on playing contact sports with men if they don't have to? And what does it mean when a woman intrudes on a formerly male-only domain?

When contact sports were dominated by a single sex, it wasn't very complicated. A man taught you how to play a manly sport, and if you qualified—that is, if you played the sport well, with skill—other men thought of you as a role model, the type of man they'd like to be.

This is completely subverted when a woman plays contact sports. Does her (male) coach attempt to teach her how to be a man? Is this integral to the sport? Should women play on women-only teams? Or does this encourage other problems? How did we get here, anyway?

One writer argues that because female athletes have always been suspected of lesbianism, the integration of genders in sport assumed great importance in the middle of the twentieth century, with physical education teachers stressing co-ed recreation rather than female sport, and privileging individual sports for women over team sports. (Cahn, 175) Men, then, were expected to play recreational sports with women (humor them) while saving their serious stuff for male-only sports and male-only teams. Failed heterosexuality—that is, homosexuality—was linked with exclusively female environments. Thus, the all-girls sports team became more and more a thing of the past. But the equivalent for men—all-male teams being suspected of homosexuality—did not come to pass, perhaps because of the almost hysterical insistence on all-male sports and all male-teams being "all man" with any hint of homosexuality firmly, even violently, suppressed.

Historian Susan K. Cahn points out that throughout history, "restrictions on physical contact continued to distinguish women's play from men's." (221) Gender-specific rules continue to ensure this differentiation within a given sport. Thus, women's feats cannot easily be compared with men's. For instance, in ice hockey, the women's rules prohibit intentional body checking. Therefore, the game is seen, even by its participants, as a somewhat inferior version of the real game, which would be the one played by men.

One hockey-playing grandmother even lectured me about this: "If you are writing about women's hockey, there is no need to compare it to men's." She goes on to point out that "I have had a lot of support from male hockey players who helped secure ice, coached, and gave clinics. In general they enjoyed coaching us women because we are so intent on listening and eager to learn." With a twinkle in her eye obvious even though we're communicating via email, she says, "'Skating like your grandma' has a new meaning since I scored in my grandson's (father-son) game." (Monson) Even though she clearly wants to emphasize the competitive and recreational nature of women-only hockey teams, she cannot resist the urge to point out that she can play on men's teams—the "real" game—as well.

Another hockey player says:

*I know plenty of people who have complained about the growth of women's hockey ... saying it's slower, less fun to watch, or not worth the money it takes. But any time women take on a predominantly male sport, it's not going to look or be the same as when men do it. We are going to do it the best we can, and perform the best we can, within our limits. Women may have less upper body strength, that doesn't necessarily mean the game will be slower, just played with more finesse. Checking isn't allowed in women's hockey, so there is automatically less hitting, which is one major pull for the public to watch hockey. However, there is plenty of body contact, riding off into the boards. Women's hockey is not a pansy sport. ... We sweat just as much, push, shoot and pass just as hard.* (Wellman)

The women who try to explain the attraction of women-only teams almost always sound a little defensive. They have heard all the arguments about how the women's game compares unfavorably to the men's, so they want to be clear that we are talking about two different things: men's game, women's game. At the same time, they don't want spectators or observers to assume that the women's game is inferior, so they must identify ways in which the game as played by women is actually superior to the one played by men. Not surprisingly, almost every woman I interviewed reported playing with or against men, at least informally (exceptions were mostly football players). Also not surprisingly, most of them relish the experience of playing the "real" sport.

This is not to say that women are obsessed with competing with men or comparing their athletic achievements to men's. As sportswriter Nelson points out, "The act of sport remains a human act, unrelated to gender. There is nothing male about throwing a ball or practicing lay-ups. There are long moments when women athletes do not feel the presence of men. Entire games are played, entire races run in which women never think of men." (6)

Women in contact sports who compete with men have very good reasons for doing so. Most martial artists and boxers insist that the only way they get better is by training with men. Yet the idea of women competing directly with men is unappealing to some observers, frightening to others, and for still others, titillating. The male/female contact is eroticized. (Sekules 84) This is not helped by marketing efforts that focus on the voyeuristic qualities of watching women compete. Nevertheless, it is important to continue the work of integration, believes Deborah Slaner Larkin, the former executive director of the Women's Sports Foundation. "Separate is never equal," she says. (Zimmerman, 92) Sportswriter Nelson echoes this comment: "Is separate but equal ever equal?" she asks. (86)

One martial artist says, "We [martial artists] have been competing against men from day one. I've never felt awkward about it. There are some men who kick hard, and I'm wary of them. However, this is the same with some women." (Stambaugh) A teenage football player says, "When I played, [the boys] wanted to take me out. They were rude, but I survived. I don't like playing a sport where you just stand there." (Albright)

A martial artist says,

*In my particular sport, competing against men is a must. With the self-defense part of Tae Kwon Do, one must have a sense of what a man would do if he attacked you. Who better to learn from than a male! Since I have never given much thought to what people say, if they had concerns, it did not get expressed to me.* (Robinson)

A hockey player recalls her childhood experiences playing hockey with boys: "The boys always commandeered the ice, so if you wanted to skate, you had to play." (Lentz) This exchange is common even when women reach adulthood. There are not as many opportunities for women to play on women-only teams, so they opt for the mixed gender version, or they decide to be the only woman on a formerly all-male team.

A football player explains how she enjoys playing football with men but is often reluctant to do so:

*I do play some pickup ball against men. Most of them are either family or friends. The first time we play is usually the most fun. Most guys have it in them that they are better, and then they get beat, especially by a girl, it destroys them. Then they either never play with us again or they play nasty, taking cheap shots. I prefer not to play with them but only because it ruins more friendships than I gain.* (Walsh)

Women report mixed reactions from men. Many of them have received only grudging support from men. A martial artist says:

*I was the only woman in my dojo* [training hall] *and I kept going until I was the highest ranking member and all the men ahead of me had dropped out.* [The men] *didn't like it very much, often thinking I was less regardless of how good I became. ... After a while, they knew they didn't have the same motivation to be good, and they learned to respect my abilities.* (Bunker)

In some cases, men feel less threatened by female competitors than one might expect. One boxer comments on the reactions she gets from men: "Men [who] aren't involved in any kind of boxing or martial arts, they tend to humor you. Like, 'Oh, how cute, she can punch.' The ones in martial arts or boxing, they just see you as a comrade: 'You box? Oh cool.'" (McCaughey, 128) Another boxer concurs: "Guys in the gym are accepting except for the immature young ones [whom she identifies as college students]. ... I had suspected that the men at the boxing gym might resent the presence of women, but they actually seem quite glad the women are there." (McCaughey, 128)

Not all male athletes react that way, however. A martial artist relates how "a few instructors didn't like women in the sport and said so. But over time, there has been a change in attitude—people really accept women in sports. It wasn't always like that." (Dumin). It still isn't always like that

Outsiders don't know how to react to them, these women commonly report. "People in general seem to assume it's much more macho than it really is," one hockey player says. She also goes on to say, "My husband loves that I play. He especially likes when I play with the men. I think he finds it sexy in a tough, macho kind of way." (Kangas, P.)

When girls play with boys and women with men, they play people who are in general more advanced, in terms of skill, more aggressive and more willing to take the initiative. Girls and women then learn to incorporate these skills into their own playing. Girls who only play with other girls and women who only play with women are at a demonstrable disadvantage. Still, competition between women and men is often suppressed or discouraged, occasionally by the players themselves.

A football players says she occasionally scrimmages with men, "but they don't want to hit a girl." (Poehler) A hockey player says, "I've had men after a game refuse to shake my hand (one guy still does that ten years after I started playing against him!)" (McDowell)

A rugby player who practices with a men's team says:
*99% of the team thinks it is great. ... I have some dissension from one player about 'no women on his field'... but the rest of the guys have backed me. ... The only funny part has been in practice, no matter what, eventually I will take a hit, be in the wrong place, or get groped inadvertantly by one of the guys. ... They are the only ones that notice. I am there to*

*play, not worry about if they got a handful while running a drill* (Park).

She goes on to say that the women's team she's developing lacks the intensity of the men's and has arranged for them to practice with the men "to develop a better group of women." (Park)

About the drawbacks of playing with men, one hockey player says:

*It was extremely difficult (and still is most of the time) to keep up with the guys I played with. I had to learn quick. I had to do everything 10 times better than everyone else or I'd never get any passes or any ice time. ... I am the only girl who plays competitively at [my] rink. Let me tell you just how hard it is, some days, to face those guys. If I do well, they don't like it because I may have made them look bad. If I do poorly, I'm either just proving them right (I don't belong there) or pissing them off if they're on my team. And I make a superb scapegoat when we lose. ... However, it's not all that bad. ... Guys who are confident in themselves respect me and my efforts to better my playing. Some respect me for it, some play with me like they would any guy. But some just hate me there and go out of their way to rough me up. I've gotten two concussions and two broken noses playing hockey and it wasn't necessarily because the guys liked me. ... The better the player the guy is, the more tolerant he will be of me. Guys who aren't as good, I think they feel threatened by any skill I may have. What guy wants some girl to come out and show him up?* (Wellman)

Another hockey player reports a slightly more welcoming reception from her male teammates and competitors in the men's league:

*I took learning to play seriously and was usually the only woman in the hockey classes offered at local rinks. I caught on quickly and became good enough to be invited to play in the Senior 'Men's' hockey league. I was the first woman in Lansing to do this and my reception was overwhelmingly positive with a few sceptics scattered throughout the league. Incredibly ... our team won the championship! I became the first woman to skate over and receive the "Manly" Cup!* (Wiechers).

"Where teams are truly co-ed, that's great. But when a team is only co-ed because you're on it, that's not so great," one hockey player warns. "The only girl has to be pretty good to be accepted by boys. For similar reasons, I don't play against men under 30. They still have too much to prove and I'm not interested in their manliness." (Kangas, P.)

Men can find the process of competing against women difficult; they fear losing to women, they fear hurting women; they operate under the delusion that striking a woman's breast is a mortal wound. All of these concerns are legitimate. But they can be overcome. Why should men want to compete against women? Because they do so in all other arenas anyway. Because it is healthy for them to get a sense of what women can do. And it is healthy for them to stop relating to women only in terms of their gender. Instead, when women compete against men, everyone can win. Your opponent or your partner can simply be an opponent or a partner. The fact of his or her maleness or femaleness doesn't have to be relevant.

A martial artist says she liked competing against men, that her teacher "didn't discriminate between men and women. There was no gender in the dojang [training hall]. The men in class always treated me with respect," she says. "The women in class didn't give up. ... We pushed harder to compete with the men and we certainly didn't get any breaks." (Friesen)

Another martial artist who competes regularly with men says:

*At first some intimidated me and some annoyed the heck out of me. One in particular made comments and almost made me quit until I realized this person was stupid and made stupid comments to everyone. ... I used to always interrupt the fighting to ask questions about what I was doing until a male sparring partner looked me in the eye and said, "Shut up and spar." I stopped feeling lost and apologetic after that. ... Overall, everyone was really encouraging and competing with men became a lot of fun. I learned that guys don't necessarily have an advantage even if they had a sports background. I saw a lot of guys who didn't do as well as I did. ... And everyone starting out looks as bad as I did.* (Anderson, V.)

One hockey player explains the drawbacks of competing with men: "Some guys refuse to pass to you, or just tell you to leave right to your face, that you don't belong here, it's a guy's sport, things along those lines." Why does she continue to compete with men? She explains it this way: "Playing with them, though, and standing up to them, it's a high for me. I love to be able to put a guy who thinks he's unstoppable in his place." She feels compelled to add, "I'm not a man-hater ... but I don't like being told what I cannot do. I want the chance, I want to score just as bad as he does." (Wellman)

Another hockey players claims that she has "never had a negative experience playing with men." Of course, she adds, it "helps that I could always hold my own out on the rink, but I never heard anyone complain that 'a girl' was playing. I must admit I always enjoyed taking out some of the better/bigger guys and hearing them be razzed by their teammates since I was 'a girl.'" (Waddell-Rutter)

A martial artists says, "Generally [male sparring partners] were quite gentle in the beginning . ... But usually they understood fairly quickly that I was serious about what I was doing and if they didn't give it their all, then they weren't doing me any favors." (Troutwine)

One hockey player ruminates on her male teammates and opponents:

*It's hard to say how guys feel about me on the ice. ... Guys on my own team have said things like, "Damn woman goalie"if I'm not playing well. (Usually when they're not playing well, either!) But these comments have come from people with little respect for their teammates anyway.* (Torrance)

She describes an incident when she subbed as a goalie on a higher level team:

*The guys were just thrilled to have a goalie, so the gender issue didn't matter. ... The other team wasn't so pleased, though* [no women play regularly in the league]. *A member of the opposing team crashed the net and knocked me down. I was out for a few seconds ... and when I got up I was pretty dizzy. ... I thought it was an isolated event ... but another female goalie has had similar situations and maybe I'm not so sure it was an isolated event anymore. Anyway, I continued the game. ... I was not about to look weak or give anyone a reason to look down on women playing at this level. ... [My] team really stepped up the roughness of the game after I got hit. ...What I didn't expect was for several of the other team's players to actually apologize to me and say that that guy was out of line.* (Torrance)

She relates that men have "a fair amount of surprise if they can't score on me easily. ... They say, 'Gee, I couldn't get anything by you all night.' I don't know but I don't think they say that to male goalies." (Torrance)

Another woman relates a similar story:

*The men's league I play in has been getting rougher ... I was tackled from behind during a game — I wasn't even on the puck. I reached out and tripped him. He got the penalty. He was incensed, called me all sorts of names.* [Her voice shakes as she continues the story.] *He said, "You don't belong here, go play in the women's league."* (Lentz)

"You don't belong here" gets said to these women a lot.

She goes on to describe her reaction: "He couldn't have said anything more devastating, although my team kept saying, 'You do belong on this team.'" She says it was the main reason she quit playing in the men's league. "It didn't matter how good I was, they would think I didn't belong there. No matter what." (Lentz) She does say that "sometimes opponents would compliment my play and encourage me to continue." She plays in a woman's league only now and says, "I'm now more of a role model—one of the best players. I can hone my skills rather than just stay alive. I'm faster in this league and can work on stick handling." (Lentz)

A hockey player who played in boys' leagues all her life says, "I almost always felt as if I was just part of the team. ... It was with these boys I was able to score the game-tying goal with seconds left to help my team go on to become the State Consolation Champions ... and gain a feeling of great pride that probably encouraged me to stick with it" (Ward). She also played on her high school's boys' team and relates a memorable experience:

*As the only girl in the entire league, word had gotten out. Every so often I would run against a guy who thought it was really macho to* try *to hurt me. ... In this particular game ... a boy was throwing elbows at my head and checking me as if he was attempting to split me in half. My coach pulled me aside ... [and] gave me these instructions: "If that guy hits you one more time when you don't have the puck, I want you to two-hand him with your stick as hard as you can. We will take the penalty." The very next shift*

*out, the same boy ... threw an elbow .... I did as I was in-*
*structed ... and as he turned, my adrenaline began to flow*
*full force and while he was busy throwing every "sissy"*
*comment and vulgarity at me, I threw a hard right hook ...*
*and my first (and so far last) fight had begun. I didn't know*
*if the ref was going to be able to pull me off because he was*
*laughing so hard. For the first time, I had earned the re-*
*spect of the boys* [on her team], *the coach, and our oppo-*
*nents. I don't remember if I ever did see the ice again that*
*night, but that did not matter. What mattered was the feel-*
*ing of acceptance in this male-dominated sport.* (Ward)
Another younger player says:

*I took hockey as a Physical Education class and was one of*
*two girls in the class of about 30. ... A few of them always*
*said how cool it was and wanted to be on my team when we*
*scrimmaged. I don't know if they thought it was a novelty*
*or genuinely were glad to see women playing, but either*
*way it was nice to be respected on the ice.* (Kangas, G.)

Others have expressed similar feelings of acceptance: "On
one particular game, we had a small bench. ... I tried to sit
between two of my players and said, 'Move over, let the lady
have a seat.' One of the players said, 'You're not a lady, you're
a hockey player.' That actually made me feel good."
(Grabowski)

Another hockey player says, succinctly, "I like to play with
women for one kind of challenge and camaraderie and men for
another. I wouldn't voluntarily give up either." (Kangas, P.)

One woman who has been playing hockey since her youth
says that for the most part, she is welcomed by men, and that
those men who do not welcome her are set straight by the men
who do:

*I was very self-conscious to be a girl playing a "boys'" game.*
*... I gained a lot of experience and confidence by playing*

[women's] *college hockey and never felt self-conscious about playing with men after college. Instead of "hiding" the fact that I played and loved playing, I was proud of the fact that I played and was good enough to play with men. Most of the men I play with really like having me play ... and are very supportive. I have definitely run into men/boys who don't like having a woman on the ice, but they are by far the minority. And the men who support me playing are not afraid to make it clear to the "non-supporters" that I am more welcome than they are.* (Hallada-Pinhey)

Most men, one hockey player says, "showed a great deal of respect, but not 'special' treatment. They shot the puck just as hard as they would have on a guy, but they never tried to take runs at me or hurt me." (Formosa)

Another, agreeing that her male teammates have been very supportive of her, describes this experience:

*Our team captain (of all people) apparently thought women belonged barefoot and pregnant. He would pick on me in the locker room ... stand there and watch* [the opposing team] *go in on me on a breakaway ... and then blame me if they scored. I had a huge fight with him over it and then told our team manager it was him or me. Well, our team manager chose me ... So it was nice to get that support and have that jerk told to hit the road—his attitude wasn't needed.* (Formosa)

But these women have fought their battles privately. On the public stage, the stakes seem higher and the opposition more brutal. In a bout that drew more criticism than praise, Margaret MacGregor fought a sanctioned boxing match against Loi Chow—the first professional boxing match to take place between a woman and a man—in Seattle in October 1999 and won in a four round unanimous decision. (Sekules, 234) "The battle of the sexes is on," the newspaper reports proclaimed, because of course any athletic competition between men and women must somehow signal a larger, corresponding cultural meaning. It can't just be two athletes competing.

Loi Chow said that he knew people would call him a wimp if he lost and a brute if he won, but he still participated in the match. He said, "Regrets—I have none." And went on to say, "She is not a woman the moment she steps in the ring with me. When she steps in the ring with me, she's an opponent." ("Man vs. Woman")

To the annoying media attention, MacGregor said, "I'm just a small-town girl. I like to box. You all got pretty excited." To critics, she said, "I think they should open their minds a little more." ("Man vs. Woman") Critics included organizations such as the International Female Boxers Association, which called the match "a terrible sideshow." (International Female Boxers Association website)

Whatever the reporters might have to say, women competing with and against men in contact sports is here to stay. It is even becoming less and less remarkable. Breann Smith, a junior on the Ann Arbor Pioneer High School football team, made a three-yard touchdown run in a game in September 1999, one of a few touchdowns scored by female football players in the past several years. Her coach, Pat Fox, said, "She's worked hard ... and it was her turn to carry the ball. We don't treat her any differently and she doesn't want to be treated any differently. She's a competitor and a fantastic athlete." ("Touchdown")

A wrestling coach describes coaching his co-ed teams with gender being "immaterial." In his state, there are no girls' teams, so the girls wrestle the boys. He talks about a girl on another team who recently took third place at a regional tournament. "She did really super against the boys," he says, "a super, super job." He credits her mental edge and quickness and points out that she comes from a long line of (male) wrestlers. The girls he coaches practice the same as the boys, are part of the team, doing whatever the boys do. "They always just do it," he says of the girls on his teams. "And they expect to be treated the same." The matches are judged the same no matter who is wrestling, he says, and the guidelines don't change. "But some teams ... the boys would rather take the forfeit than wrestle girls. When boys refuse to wrestle girls it's one of two things. Either they consider it a lose-lose situation—if you win, you beat a girl, if you lose, you lost to a girl, so they can't see the point—or it is not their choice. A principal or coach will tell them they can't compete against girls." He pauses and adds with some pride, "My boys would never take the forfeit." (Anderson, B.)

Women are even joining men in the locker room—not as journalists or broadcasters, but as teammates. One hockey player says,

*I have evolved to insisting on joining my men's team in the locker room. There are very divided camps on this among the women I know who play with men. I think it's important and it makes me feel part of the team. A lot of the game is not played on the ice, but develops between the team members off the ice. I feel it also helps my game to hear all the "play by play" after the game. Generally, there are a few men who are bothered at first but they get over it (or be quiet about it, which is just as good). (Kangas, P.)*

Another player who also changes with the men says, "They treat me like I'm one of them." (Lentz) But another hockey player points out a difficulty she encounters:

*Wives/girlfriends of players [can be] really upset that I'm in the locker room with their significant (male) other. ... There's something very titillating to some people about the possibility of having someone of the opposite sex in the locker*

*room. I don't shower with the team ... so I'm never nude in front of [them] but I have had some very aggressive, very angry women accost me with how inappropriate it is for me to be in the same room as their, presumably fully naked, spouse. (Ironically, usually their spouse is very discreet). ... Sometimes it hurts more since it comes from a woman.* (McDowell)

For these women, fully participating in the sport means playing with men and forcing men to confront their own stereotypes about women. They truly feel gender is irrelevant. They aren't in the locker room because they want to see naked men. They're in the locker room because they're part of the team.

Not everyone thinks women and men should—or even *can*—play or compete with each other. One of the most destructive beliefs most people, including athletes, have is the belief that men are innately superior to women in physical abilities. As Colette Dowling has shown in her landmark study, *The Frailty Myth,* men's "superior" physical abilities are a matter of environment more than genetics. Male children are expected to develop physical skills whereas female children are not. Martha McCaughey calls this routine and systematic suppression of girls' and women's physical abilities "de-skilling" and says that "girls are still discouraged from participating in sports, particularly those that involve rough play or competitiveness. The cultivation of ... fighting skills still counts as unfeminine." (42) As sociologist Nancy Theberge says, it is "difficult to transcend traditional assumptions that differences between the sexes are biological rather than cultural." (139) And, as McCaughey relates, "what is usually taken for granted as a fact of nature—that a woman simply cannot physically challenge a man—is revealed as a social script which privileges men at the expense of women." (7) Sportswriter Mariah Burton Nelson says, "Despite the fitness boom of the 80s, women remain to a large degree physically uneducated, even retarded. Their competence has been slowed, delayed; their physical proficiency has been hindered." (28) Lower expectations for women, she believes, "lead to inferior performance and, perhaps most damaging, to a belief on the part of both girls and boys that boys are naturally superior athletes." (33)

It is hard for men and women to believe that women can engage in a fair fight with men, a fight between equals. One martial artist says, "Men tend to think of women as weaker and less equal." As sparring partners, she says, "It was hard to get past their reluctance to treat me as an equal partner." (Troutwine) At the same time, a hockey player points out, "I like to play with men because they're mostly bigger than me so I don't feel bad about hitting them. The women are usually smaller than me so I kind of hold back." (Kangas, P.)

A football player says, "I believe that a pro football league can be nothing but a good thing. It throws into question the assumption that only men can be tough and competitive. ... Why shouldn't girls have something like the pros to which to aspire? Doesn't the very dream, the goal, and the possibility of it becoming reality build character, drive and self-esteem?" (Noah)

Women can learn all of the skills they need to succeed in athletics; it would help if they learned them at a young age the way that men do. The brain plasticity that helps you learn motor skills quickly begins to decline by the time people become teenagers, so the time to start learning sports is at a young age.

Women and men are more equivalent physically than has been believed. In fact, the gap between world records for men and women has fallen considerably in the last decade as more and more women begin participating in sports at a younger age and thus train their bodies for success. As sportswriter

Nelson says, "Comparing women with men is an imprecise science partly because researchers have usually compared trained men with untrained women." (41) As more women become trained, physical differences between men and women will probably become less obvious, and that nature of those differences, if any, will become clearer.

Sports historian Allen Guttmann confirms this perspective when he says:

> *When the women of* this *historical moment sit quietly at home with their knitting while the women of* that *time and place battle their muddy way through the travail of a rugby tournament, differences in social structure and in culture offer a more likely explanation than any suggested by physiology.* (4)

For most of these women, participating in a contact sport and competing against men helps them realize that some women have greater physical skills than some men and some men have greater physical skills than some women. But contact sports aren't simply about who's biggest or strongest, who's capable of being biggest or strongest. They are also about skill, technical accuracy, agility, speed and flexibility. Of these qualities necessary for success, women have many advantages.

This assessment isn't shared by all women, of course. One martial artist says, "I secretly admire the girls who go out for baseball, wrestling and football, to name a few male-dominated sports. Obviously they can only advance so far before they are naturally eliminated or excluded." (Cox) To some observers, this is indeed "obvious"; to others, it is not.

Sports journalists point out that when women play men in contact sports, it is usually because they are either challenging a male-only preserve—asking why men should have all the fun—or they don't have any choice. There isn't any female competition (no programs for girls and women) or else the level of competition is lacking. The women in contact sports agree. A hockey players says, "I appreciate the fact that I can play with other women. But if a woman's team wasn't around, I'd be playing right alongside the guys." (Waddell-Rutter)

But what journalists sometimes miss is that women also compete against men because the rules are different. In basketball, women play a different game, even using a different ball, than men do. In women's ice hockey, organizers adopted a no-body-checking policy in the late 1980s that became widespread; in 1992, international women's hockey leagues also adopted the no-body-checking policy. Players bemoan the loss of body-checking, feeling it's an integral part of the game—as indeed it is. In some mixed gender leagues, body-checking is allowed. A number of adult women players played in boys' leagues, where body-checking is allowed, and they note a distinct difference between men's and women's hockey. (Theberge 1)

In an article on Angela Ruggiero, defenseman for US Olympic Hockey, sportswriter Michael Farber says:

*Of course* [she] *has been playing in manacles since she joined the national team five years ago. Although she has quick feet, a developing shot and a keen hockey sense, she is only allowed to operate with perhaps 75% of her gifts. She is the most physically dominant player in a game that doesn't permit body checks: a 5' 9" defenseman with an NHL body.*(94)

Ruggiero herself says, "I would want to play with checking. I'd be so dominant if I could use my physical presence instead of being penalized for it." (Farber 94)

Sociologist Theberge, who followed a woman's ice hockey team for several years, says, "Conventional wisdom [says] that great sport [is] men's sport and ... women are intruders in the world of sport." (1) Men's sports are privileged over women's sports. (112) This being that case, of course women want to play men's sports. If women's sports are inferior, and you want to be a superior athlete, you want to play the superior sport.

One hockey player shares why she likes to play with men: "In general, they play a faster and harder game—mostly because there are more guys who played hockey as kids than women. ... In order to get in enough ice time, I need to play with men, too." She goes on to share her ambivalence about her role:

> *If I'm not playing well, I don't really want the opposing*
> *team to know I'm a woman because I don't want them to*
> *think, "Oh, that's because their goalie's a woman." But if*
> *I'm playing well, I make a point of taking my helmet off to*
> *shake hands to say, "See, women can play this game, too!"*
> *I know that's pretty shallow.* (Torrance)

She also echoes a common sentiment of female athletes playing men, "I really don't want the guys to play any differently because I'm a woman. ... I'd rather take the killer slap shots than know that people were holding back because I'm a woman." (Torrance)

"I really love being treated as an equal," says a martial artist about competing with men. "And sometimes have been regarded as an adversary." (Wensel)

Should women play against men in contact sports? Should women fight men, so to speak? Or should the genders remain separate? The answer, most experts believe, is some combination of both. Women who train and work with men gain certain advantages—and men who train and work with women also gain certain advantages. There are risks, of course, in pitting men against women. "We train with males," says one martial artist. "In fact, I've attended classes where I was the only female present. ... Friends and family members were very concerned when my male sparring partner kicked me and broke one of my ribs." But this did not stop her from continuing her training. (Cox) There are risks in all contact sports. A football player points out that she was injured early in her first year of playing on a women-only team, at a time when she was inexperienced. Since then, her only injury has been a minor sprained ankle. (Noah)

Alleviating risk is practiced in most sports by pairing people of similar ability together, or of separating men from women. This sometimes shortchanges women because the best way to get better is to compete with someone who is better than you are, and often those people are men. But not always. A hockey player says, "[When] novice women [join] the sport, many of them do not welcome the advanced players and it is inappropriate for us to play competitively with them." (Hallada-Pinhey)

Like many athletes, she believes the main way to alleviate risk is to teach people how to play the sport properly. Then, man or woman, man against women, the risk of injury is reduced. "Ideally," says sportswriter Nelson, "sports would be organized not according to gender but according to height, weight and skill level." (52) This approach is based on a "partnership" model of sports participation that many female sports leaders advocate.

As Nelson concludes, "You can't be a female athlete without addressing questions of femininity, sexuality, fear, power, freedom and just how good you are compared to men." (196)

## Chapter Six
## Why People Disapprove

In May, 2000, Hugh Hefner hosted an evening of prize fighting, televised on ESPN2, at the Playboy Mansion, complete with Miss November boxing Miss Hawaiian Tropic. As a reporter wrote, "Bunnies pranced, canoodled and cavorted, among them women like Paulette Myers, a veteran of five Playboy special edition issues." An onlooker commented that one of the boxers was there only "because she looks good," and as the reporter dryly put it: "Isn't everybody?" (Walters)

The boxing match at the Playboy Mansion sums up everything undesirable about women and contact sports—at least for women seriously interested in competing in contact sports. It also gives observers ammunition in their opposition to women's participation in contact sports. The Playboy match even demonstrates to perfection the tiresome practice of conflating women's sports, particularly contact sports, with sexuality and titillation.

In another instance of the juxtaposition of women in contact sports with sexuality, in researching this book, I had the opportunity to investigate the sedately titled "Women's International Sports Clubs," which, in my innocence, I took to be clubs that supported the cause of women in sports. In fact, these clubs actually produce "catfight" and topless wrestling videos and offer mixed wrestling opportunities for male members. How disappointing.

Eroticizing women in contact sports is one way to put women in their place. It eliminates the possibility that women could seriously compete, that they could want to play a contact sport as an athlete. It trivializes their desire to work hard at their chosen sport.

Eroticizing women in contact sports is not the only—or even the most—effective method for excluding women from contact sports. But the purpose is clear. Many people don't want women to seriously pursue excellence in contact sports. In her study of gender and sexuality in sport, *Coming on Strong*, Susan K. Cahn points out that attempts to keep women from participating in men's sports is an attempt to "preserve gender differences." (25) In the 1920s and 1930s, she shows, female athletes bested male athletes, beating world record times and otherwise showing themselves as equal or superior in many areas of sports. Athletic leaders responded by resisting any further attempts by changing the rules for women and prohibiting direct competition between men and women. (52) Why? Perhaps because women proving themselves strong and capable in sport "might also signal a loss of masculine privilege and superiority." (32)

As the feminist scholar Martha McCaughey points out in *Real Knockouts: The Physical Feminism of Women's Self-Defense*, "aggression is a primary marker of sexual difference ... aggression is one way we culturally tell men and women apart." (2 - 3)

If sports make men masculine, then what happens when women become competitive? Certainly women athletes are frequently criticized as being masculine or mannish, but more than that, women's participation in sports calls into question whether sports can "prove" that men are masculine. If women can play a given sport, how can the men competing in the sport be proving their masculinity? Men who participate in contact sports are almost virulently anti-homosexual (at least in public; who knows what may go on in their private lives?) If contact sports became the province of women—and femininity—what might this mean? Athletic contact, then, as historian Cahn points out, could "conceivably intimate homosexuality" for men. (218) If participating in contact sports challenges our ideas of what is feminine—women punch each other, punch men, and are still women, can still be wives and mothers—then their participation must challenge what masculinity is. And what is masculine is as fragile as what is feminine. (Dowling, 22)

"The presence of powerful women athletes [strikes] at the roots of male dominance in American society," Cahn speculates. (207-208) Perhaps this is why women's contact sports, especially boxing, have been derided, particularly in the boxing press. (Sekules, 131)

Even Joyce Carol Oates, ordinarily a friend of women, in a jeremiaid in *On Boxing*, says, "Men fighting men to determine worth ... excludes women as completely as the female experience of childbirth excludes men. ... In any case, raw aggression is thought to be the peculiar province of men, as nurturing is the peculiar province of women. (The female boxer violates this stereotype and cannot be taken seriously—she is parody, she is cartoon, she is monstrous. Had she an ideology, she is likely to be a feminist.) ... Boxing is for men, and is about men, and *is* men." (Sekules, 54-55) Get the picture?

In case you didn't, sports columnist Bill Gallo has this to say: "Women are too precious and tender a commodity to have their faces butchered and bashed as they make utter fools of themselves." (Zimmerman, 197) I would allege that if getting your face butchered and bashed makes you an utter fool, than male boxers ought also to be discouraged, although not because they are "too previous and tender a commodity." Note the word "commodity"? Women aren't objects, they are people. They are allowed to choose whether they want to get their faces butchered and bashed.

Bryant Gumbel, reporting on the first women's professional boxing match, called it "an inferior product." (Sekules, 162) Again, the emphasis on "product" seems parallel to the idea of woman as "commodity." A woman competing in a boxing match isn't concerned with packaging a product, at least not primarily. She is concerned about winning a match. If a spectator conceives of a sport as a commodity, a product, he or she is missing the point.

One promoter defends female boxers, saying "People say this is a gimmick. But when the gloves are put on, it's no gimmick." ("Falling in Line") This is a relatively lone voice in the wilderness. This lack of support may be because so much information about women in sports is, in sportswriter Mariah Burton Nelson's words, "filtered through male writers, photographers, broadcasters and publishers. [About 10,000 or 95%] of the nation's print and broadcast sports journalists are men." (6)

A bias against female athletes has always existed; it is particularly virulent when directed against women who participate in violent sports. People still think there's something "socially wrong" with female athletes. (Zimmerman, 28) One who participates in a contact sport must really be an outcast. One martial artist reacts to this disapproval with a dismissive: "They should get with the times. Women can do anything they want." (Bove)

But not everyone agrees. When I was training for my black belt, a martial arts magazine carried this headline: "Do Women

Belong in the Training Hall?" I remember shaking with anger just seeing the headline, let alone reading the article. This was 1994, after all. I couldn't believe that the question could even be asked. But that was before I realized that observers—men and women alike—think that men are in serious pursuit of excellence when they participate in sports, whereas women are just hobbyists, or, worse, looking for a partner. (Zimmerman, 28) Ironically, I know of a dozen or more romantic partnerships that have stemmed from women's involvement in contact sports. This isn't because that women set out to find men, but rather that women who are involved in contact sports find that men involved in contact sports understand and respect them in a way that outsiders find difficult.

One of the most pernicious ways that disapproval prevents women from participating in sports is when it is translated into an alleged concern for their health. The paternalism that allows men to box, for instance, but not women, is particularly galling to women in contact sports. Women historically have been warned of the "perceived health dangers of aggressive competition," (Cahn, 26) the implication being that they're too weak to play. The belief that physical exertion hurts women is still prevalent today. (Zimmerman, 28) In Britain, where Jane Couch sued the Amateur Boxing Association in order to force the group to sanction female amateurs, the British Medical Association called the decision, "a demented extension of equal opportunities." (Sekules, 76) The medical community has always resisted the participation of women in sports, particularly competitive sports or contact sports. The prevailing myth—which still holds sway today—is that women are frail, as compared to men.

When I was a child, I used to run and lift and play just like my brother did. One summer, when I was about 9 or 10, all of that changed. I was helping my father build a rock retaining wall. It was my job to carry rocks from the driveway to the backyard. I thought this was a fantastic job, although I realize now that my father had duped me: he didn't feel like carrying all the rocks from the driveway to the backyard. My mother, however, put a stop to this almost immediately. I was growing up, she said, and couldn't do things like that anymore. She couldn't exactly articulate why not, but she intimated that "you could get hurt down there," down there being the nether regions we never talked about—my reproductive organs. It was the first time I was ashamed of being a girl.

My father did not challenge my mother; didn't she know best? In fact, she had merely bought into an old wives' tale—or, rather, an old doctors' tale—that women who exerted themselves jeopardized their ability to reproduce. That was the threat, the punishment that hung over women who wanted to invade the male domain: the punishment for physical activity was, as Dowling expresses it, "the loss of their capacity to bear children." (3) Sports historian Allen Guttmann points out that in addition to risking infertility, historically, female athletes were warned that they risked madness and early death. (95)

Women who view themselves as athletes and have little concern about whether they are viewed as feminine are roundly criticized by observers. Cahn asks, "And why [do] observers, especially the fraternity of male sportswriters, find it so disturbing when a small group of women [place] athletic goals ahead of standard notions of 'feminine beauty'?" (207) A martial artist says, "Most say I'm too old, too tiny, and that it will ruin my looks and my femininity if I continue. Balderdash!" (Wensel)

Almost all of the women who participate in contact sports do so despite the strong disapproval of their families. It is unladylike to get hit hard, to hit hard enough to leave a mark. It was not what our families had in mind when they sent us out into the world. Our mothers have conflicted emotions about what we do. Sports journalist Zimmerman says, "mothers as well as fathers may feel a bit discomfited when they see their daughters competing aggressively, especially in tough sports such as wrestling, football or boxing." (8)

A hockey player says:

*My mom has told me to quit a million times, afraid that I will hurt myself or get another concussion. "CAT scans aren't cheap," she says. "You want to be a vegetable for the rest of your life?" My boyfriend right now doesn't like to watch me play but he will still come to my games. I catch him wincing in the stands if someone knocks me down or punches me. ... I know he wishes I didn't play either. He has said to me many times not to bite off more than I can chew, making sure I realize that he can't help me if I get into a fight or if someone gets violent. But I know I'm on my own out there, that's what I like about it. I need my team to win and to make the play work, but I take care of myself out there. No one stands up for me but me.* (Wellman)

"A *lot* of people don't approve of women playing hockey," says one hockey player. "I no longer care on my behalf, but it annoys me because I think it discourages younger girls who might want to play." (Kangas, P.)

"There are people who disapprove of women playing hockey," agrees another player. "I don't even pay attention to it." (Hallada-Pinhey)

"Here's the question I get most," says a biomedical engineering graduate student: "You play *rugby*?' The other comment I get is, 'I didn't know women played rugby.' People are incredulous when I tell them, yes, we do tackle and yes, it is full contact. I kind of like shocking people like that. It makes me different and appear tougher. People seem impressed. That's enjoyable." (Womack) But people's reactions aren't always enjoyable.

The Infotelefon Female Football League website reports that although women's football in Germany is more advanced than elsewhere in the field, "Even today, some officials and players remain skeptical and follow the development suspiciously."

"I used to hear a lot of smartass comments," says a martial artist. "Since I am a girl, the guys would think it was really funny to say, 'You kick like a girl.' Duh. I *am* a girl." Once, when she entered a tournament in the junior division (to age 17), she competed against boys and won all three areas of competition—forms, sparring, and board breaking. When the boys discovered she was a girl (she wore her hair short and at the time had not fully developed), the boys complained to the conference organizers and forced her to compete in the girls' division—although there were no other girls competing in her age group. She was allowed to keep her medals, but the boys re-did their competition and anointed new winners in the three categories. She says, "I hear all the time how girls can't do this or that. It just makes me go that much harder." (Anderson, C.)

"What are they afraid of?" one hockey players asks. "That we'll be better at it?" (Formosa)

"Some people definitely disapprove of women playing rugby," says one player, "because it's such a rough sport. I think it's ridiculous to stop women from being involved in any sport. ... Women are just as capable of playing rough and tough sports. [They] have a higher tolerance for pain anyway," she jokes. "Gender socialization definitely restrains women from exploring contact sports. ... Many women are missing out. [Contact sports] would do wonders for many women's self-esteem." (Fancy)

Boxer Jacqui Frazier-Lyde says, "My only pressure comes from my 16-year-old son, who plays football. He doesn't mind if I fight, but I can't lose. Because, as he puts it, 'Mom, we'll have to move away if you do. The kids will embarrass me at school.'" ("This Frazier has another motivation")

One martial artist says her family "feels it is not good for someone my age because I will be 50 years old next year." (Eaden) Another, however says, "The only family member whose opinion matters, my husband, said to go for it!" (Robinson) Whether other people disapprove, she says, "I really don't care."

Another martial artist says when she started in the early 80s, "it wasn't considered 'proper' for women to be involved in contact sports. ... Men were intrigued by it, women snubbed their noses at you. It was generally OK to learn some self-defense techniques but not OK to fight." (Troutwine)

"According to my mother," says a hockey player who skated for her high school's boys' team, "there were other mothers in the stands who would carry on very loud conversations with the topic typically revolving around who would *let* their daughter play hockey. [But] I don't let any comments really go more than skin deep because there are always enough people that are supportive about it." (Ward)

Another hockey player in the boys' leagues confirms this. "The parents ... were disgusting. I can remember moms throwing Tampax at me and telling me to get off the ice" (McDowell).

Freeda Foreman says her father, the famous boxer George Foreman, "flat out doesn't like it. But I do have his love and support. That's what counts." ("Falling in Line")

By and large, the disapproval of friends and family members—the people closest to these women—stems from concerns about physical risks. One hockey players dismisses such concerns: "I'm not worried any more about a daughter getting hurt playing a contact sport than I would be a son. Anyone can get hurt playing sports, gender has nothing to do with it." (Wellman) A martial artist says her parents questioned the appropriateness of it for her. She started in her mid-30s and they assumed the sport was for younger women. (Anderson, V.)

A football player says:

*Most of my family just shakes their head. They are afraid of me getting hurt. Since most of the women are much bigger than me, the chances of me getting hurt are probably greater. I just reassure them that I will be fine, that* [the opponents] *have to catch me to hurt me.* (Walsh)

She goes on to say, "Skeptical people are being convinced ... that women are quite capable of playing any sport. I know a lot of men that prefer to watch women's sports because you see a greater display of talent that some of the men's sports are lacking." (Walsh)

A rugby player says, "I think my parents do worry that I'll get hurt. ... I know some girls whose parents made them quit because they thought it was too dangerous. Some friends [tell] me to be careful and not get hurt. I wonder if the male players get the same responses." (Womack)

One football players says the only person who expresses concern about her involvement in contact sports is her boss, "who didn't like my getting hurt just before I had an important client presentation." (Noah) A rugby player echoes this problem. "My boss keeps saying, 'Don't get a black eye if you have a client meeting.'" (Uzelac)

Feminists and others disapprove of women in contact sports for broader, more abstract and philosophical reasons. They believe physical violence is wrong, especially for women. In fact, one of the very successful athletes that I planned to interview for this book declined to be interviewed because, as she said, she didn't want people to think she participated in a violent sport. Even though she kicks and punches people for a living. It seems, rather, that she doesn't want to think she participates in a violent sport.

One hockey player says, "I am also a pediatric nurse who has spent years volunteering in child abuse prevention programs. ... and I am an advocate of reducing violence in our children's lives. I am a pacifist who would never raise a hand to spank a child, and I detest fighting for any reason." Without apparent irony, she goes on to say, "I am probably the toughest woman in the women's league I skate in today." (Wiechers)

One martial artist draws a distinction between "sport" fighting and other types of fighting:

*Although it is considered "violent" to fight, this* [martial arts sparring] *was fighting, but in a 'non-violent' way. Yes, we hurt each other, yes, we got hurt, yes, we sent each other flying through the air or across the floor, yes, we lived at the chiropractor's office, but it wasn't because we were intentionally hurting each other. By that I mean, I wasn't angry at my sparring partners, I wasn't wanting to hurt them... I reached a point where I know I could take care of myself* [in a street fight] *but never did I feel it was appropriate for me to display violence to anyone other than a sparring partner.* (Troutwine)

Another martial artist says, "I'm not a proponent of violence at all! I have always been a pacifist and was a card-carrying member of the peace and civil rights movements back in the 60s and 70s (and still believe in these concepts today)." She adds, fully aware of the disparity: "To be perfectly honest, though, I found great pleasure and release in making contact and practicing full-tilt." (Wensel)

Many feminists have a great deal of ambivalence about women's aggression and their capacity for violence, scarcely wanting to acknowledge that it exists. McCaughey points out that "much of feminism ... rejects the possibility that anything good could come from violence." (2) One participant disputes the notion that her boxing makes her violent: "I've noticed that there seems to be an assumption that you're a violent person, and that's bothersome. ... I enjoy [boxing] as a sport and I'm not a violent person. ... And I think I could actually be healthier than people who don't do this." (McCaughey, 131) She points out that her boxing allows her a release from anger and frustration that might otherwise be expressed in more destructive ways. A rugby player claims much the same thing: "I was able to get out all my pent-up aggression in a positive way, as opposed to bickering with my friends and study partners or brooding." (Womack)

But some feminists consider women's strength and claim to political legitimacy stems from their refusal (perhaps inability) to be violent and aggressive. Such feminists argue that women who are aggressive "have traded in their own views for men's." (McCaughey, 14)

"I've always been a bit proud that I'm able to play a 'man's' sport," says a hockey player, in seeming confirmation of this point. (McDowell) Some feminists call women's interest in violent sports "right-wing" feminism. Such women buy into the existing patriarchy and identify with masculine traits rather than feminine ones, they claim. (McCaughey, 16) Feminists frequently accuse women interested in traditionally male roles and male traits of being "male-identified." Although it is true that "male" traits such as toughness are celebrated aspects of contact sports, it is difficult to argue that something so many women call "empowering" and "liberating" can be bad or wrong or against feminist principles across the board. Not all of these women can be dupes, male-identified despisers of womanhood.

McCaughey argues that traditional feminist viewpoints position women "as virtuous, non-aggressive keepers of the moral order." (McCaughey, 23) Women are thus morally superior to men, and are considered the "custodians of life." (McCaughey, 145) In this schema, violence and aggression in women are anathema, robbing them of their claim to equal status and citizenship with men by virtue of their superior innate qualities.

Feminism that equates women with passivity and non-aggression provides a limited and constricted view of women, one that sustains and perpetuates their subordinate position, and one that promotes a false "universal woman" ideal that continues the racist, class and heterosexual assumptions that have often plagued feminist theory. (McCaughey, 146)

To women in contact sports, nonviolent feminists seem naive. They appear to perpetuate an association between masculinity and violence/aggression, which women in contact sports know is false. They also accuse these theorists of positioning women as victims, and forcing them into a constraining role as caregivers, whether this is a particular woman's inclination or not.

Jeffner Allen and other feminists theorize that such an emphasis on passivity and pacifism is part of a patriarchal system of women's nonviolence and compulsory heterosexuality. In this case, "women's fighting challenges a fundamental association between women and goodness." (McCaughey, 21)

But many feminists worry that violence simply begets more violence. Simply (perhaps simplistically) put, they fear that if women participate in contact sports, they will become as violent as men in everyday life. They fear that women's aggression will make the world a more violent place. But women in contact sports would counter such an argument by pointing out that they are not responsible for world peace and harmony. Everyone, men included, is responsible for that.

Feminist scholar Martha McCaughey goes so far as to argue that women's capacity to act aggressively or violently, as proven by their participation in contact sports, could instill in men a fear of acting violent—the idea that men are violent toward women because they can be, and that if they must fear retaliation, they might stop being so violent (152). Decoupling gender and violence, McCaughey speculates, "might make men more responsible for peace and social harmony." (179)

Observers fear that women in contact sports will be unable to keep their aggressive urges under control. While none of the women or coaches I talked to considered this a problem, one boxer has written a memoir, *Looking for a Fight,* in which she blames learning to box for her violent actions outside the ring. "I arrived at this place because I was looking for a fight," she writes, making one wonder why she thinks that boxing made her violent when she clearly felt violent to start with. (Snowden Picket, 3) "Before Gleason's [boxing gym]," she writes, "I had three options during an argument. Walk or run away, wage a war with words, or surrender and make peace. But now a fourth option has suddenly presented itself: my fists." (41 - 42) It is this fourth option that ends up distressing her. Although, of course, getting into a fist fight over spilled beer is stupid, the capacity to defend oneself is not stupid. But it must be respected and controlled. Snowden Picket admits that she could not get it under control.

To be fair, she was also trained in a way that no legitimate trainer or coach would find acceptable, thrown into the ring with boxers who were taller, heavier and possessed superior skills—all before she had the capacity to defend herself. This "brutal assault," as she calls it, is not sport, not teaching. It is criminal. She says, "I wanted to feel poweful, to take up space in the world, to stop apologizing. That I thought I could do this by learning how to fight now strikes me as ludicrous and deranged." (270) It seems, sadly, that she is apologizing still.

Of course, it is possible that Snowden Picket and others like her would never have acted aggressively if she (and they) hadn't learned how to punch, but most athletes feel that people who have difficulty containing their violence will have difficulty whether they learn a specific sport or not. The only difference is that a boxer with poor self-control can punch harder than a non-boxer with poor self-control. Could the problem of out-of-control athletes grow if more women participate in contact sports? The possibility certainly exists. This, however, does not mean that the vast majority of athletes in contact sports—even boxers—can't exercise self-restraint in the everyday world. In fact, most feel that "getting their aggressions out" on the playing field makes them less aggressive and more controlled in the everyday world.

Snowden Picket's remarks about the physical dangers of boxing (and by extension, all contact sports), however, should be heeded. Concussions, blows to the kidneys, broken ribs—all can cause lasting, even permanent damage and disability. Therefore, it is important for women to consider the possibility of injury when they begin a sport. It is imperative to realize, though, that all sports are inherently dangerous, to one degree or another, and the most dangerous sports are not necessarily the ones that appear most dangerous. Horseback riding, for example, has the highest percentage of brain-related trauma injuries of any of the sports. The risk of physical injury must be weighed by any potential athlete.

At the same time as they worry that violence will beget violence, feminists often conflate violence with oppression. "Hence, feminist trepidation about women's participation in violent sports such as rugby." says McCaughey (155) who goes on to speculate that "such a framework ... leaves out the possibility of legitimate or nonoppressive violence." (155)

What is most damning, of course, at least in the eyes of many feminists, is that women in contact sports actually enjoy the contact, the aggression, the "combat." If violence is always bad, women should not enjoy it and feminists must disapprove of it. But one's abdication of violence, as McCaughey points out, is only meaningful if one is capable of violence. (157)

However, feminists who disapprove of violence see in women's enjoyment of it a lack of conscious decision making, of conscious action, painting them as foolish, as dupes of men and male-dominated culture.

Feminists, of course, aren't the only ones who feel threatened by women's violence. Much of the disapproval and criticism of women in contact sports stems from a misguided notion that violence is masculine and that women who behave in violent ways are somehow unnatural and abnormal. McCaughey points out that "no one knows better than the girls and women who engage in aggressive contact sports what a disruption of gender their participation is to so many people." (42)

In one of my early books about martial arts, *Martial Arts for Women*, I wrote about attitudes women encounter in the training hall and the transformative effects of aggressive sport. I related a story in which I felt no shame—even a certain amount of justification—in hurting a man. Every woman who has read the book identifies with that section, if only vicariously. But one male critic chastized me for this, calling me "sexist." His theory as to why I was sexist was foggy; it was clear, however, that he was uncomfortable with my enjoyment of my own physical power, my own violent capacities and felt obligated to criticize it, to try to put a stop to it. What he did not seem to realize is that the book was written by a woman for women and that his opinion was of absolutely no interest to me and to my female readers. And what feminist theorists fail to realize is the same thing: ordinary women don't particularly care what they think.

Some women in contact sports may think of themselves as feminists, but they have little connection with academic feminists. Their arguments about women in contact sports buying into a patriarchal system ring hollow. Their worries that violence might create more violence seem innocent to women who recognize that they are often at the mercy of violent men— they started it first, these women say. Finally, they have difficulty believing that something that makes them feel physically fit, mentally focused and emotionally empowered could be just plain wrong, and just because someone with a Ph.D. after her name said so.

More compellingly, women in contact sports are criticized as being purveyors of "commodity feminism." M. Ann Hall, of the University of Alberta, recently presented a paper for the Canadian Association for the Advancement of Women and Sport and Physical Activity (CAAWS) in which she points out that women's boxing (and by extension, other contact sports) "represent[s] a cultural metaphor or barometer of change in women's sport and in feminism ... [celebrating] female muscularity and physical strength and ... female aggression." She explains:

> "Postfeminists" of the third wave explicitly define themselves against and criticize feminism of the earlier second wave, which they categorize as "victim" feminism. ... The relationship between feminism and women's sport [has changed]. Popular postfeminisms have been remade into "commodity feminism" where, for example, female fitness is sold... and boxers are marketed. At the same time, there has been a reshaping of feminism into individualism, self-growth and the commodification of everyday life, with an increasing focus on the body and women's physicality. (Hall)

In essence, "commodity feminism" might be construed as feminism taken over by corporate marketers. So-called "physical feminism"—the idea that changing the body can change the mind —becomes degraded into a self-centered extension of cultural pressure to conform to society's standards of femininity. That is, the reason to get fit is so that you will appeal to men. Incidental transformations that might take place are personal only and do not require a related commitment to work for the equality of all women. Thus, third wave feminism—feminism that can accept women in contact sports—can easily be reduced to a personal, not political or global, experience. This is a legitimate concern, one for which there are no easy answers.

Some of the disapproval of women in contact sports is owing to legitimate concerns about the darker side of sports, such as problems with coaches abusing female players. Since women's sports are controlled and dominated by male coaches, these problems aren't going to go away. In some sports, there are concerns about eating disorders—athletes have a higher proportion of these problems than non-athletes. In contact sports, women are less likely to become obsessed with eating and losing weight since in contact sports, size is acceptable. However, sometimes wrestlers and boxers embark on risky diets to get down to fighting weight, which is not a problem exclusive to women. Also, women in contact sports, where bigger is often better, may use performance enhancing drugs, such as steriods, to help them succeed. Still, while these concerns are legitimate, they shouldn't be used as a reason to discourage female athletes, since they are concerns equally valid for male athletes. Members of all sports—coaches, participants and governing bodies—must work together to address these problems.

How do women react to negative opinions of their participation in sports? Laila Ali might capture it best when she says, "If I want to do something, I just do it, I really don't care what anybody has to say." ("Another Ali") A hockey player says, "I must admit I'm very good at ignoring things I don't want to hear." (Waddell-Rutter)

Commenting on a woman playing offensive line in high school, Kansas City high school sports columnist Ivan Carter says, "And that, folks, is called progress. It wasn't that long ago when ... heck, there are places now where the idea of a girl playing football would be seen as a bad thing." Of Jessica Howard, the football player he's writing about, whom he considers a trailblazer, even if she doesn't agree, he says: "You go, girl." (Carter)

## *Chapter Seven*
# What Should Be Done?

"Girls who play sports," sports journalist Jean Zimmerman says, "tend to avoid the physical, psychological and social pitfalls of modern adolescence." (x) She speaks of drug use, depression, pregnancy, loss of self-esteem. While her focus is on girls and teenagers, this holds true for women of all ages as well. When I started martial arts, I had just quit smoking; only my participation in martial arts helped me stay smoke-free in the intervening years. Other women report similar successes. Some quit smoking, some quit drinking, some become healthier and more fit. The psychologist Mary Pipher (*Reviving Ophelia*) has called our culture "girl poisoning;" it is "woman poisoning" as well. Participating in sports gives girls and women crucial tools—confidence, self-esteem—needed to survive. Sports journalist Zimmerman goes on to say, "modern life can be frighteningly random, complex, dangerous." (8) We meet these fears and defeat them every time we train in a contact sport.

The French feminist writer, Simone de Beauvoir points out, "Not to have confidence in one's body is to lose confidence in oneself." (Zimmerman, 23) By participating in sports, becoming more sure of one's body, one becomes more sure of oneself. This is especially important when some American girls, as young as third grade, report being "on a diet." (Zimmerman, 23)

One writer has already proclaimed, "Women's boxing is in the process of moving from sideshow to serious sport. ... Women's boxing is nearing showtime. The last bastion of the male gender—the brightly lit patch of canvas where men test their brute strength, pugilistic skills and old-fashioned courage has fallen. What is left to conquer?" ("The Next Ali")

Indeed, what is left to conquer? As women gain equality with men in many areas of life, they realize that there is a missing link. That women will never achieve true equality as long as they are afraid of men. (Dowling, 224) "80% of rapes are committed by someone the victim knows," reports Dowling, who asserts that we cannot achieve freedom from fear until we learn to protect ourselves (253). And learning to hit and get hit is part of freedom from fear. Yes, it would be nice if we didn't have to accommodate a culture of violence. But it exists, and if we aren't going to be oppressed by it, we have to learn to live in it.

McCaughey, relating an experience in martial arts, says, "My [martial arts] instructor simply treated us as though we did not have a fear of fighting, a fear of getting hurt, a lack of entitlement or a lack of self-esteem." (80) While McCaughey seems genuinely distressed by this experience, most women in contact sports say that this is just what they are looking for. A coach who treats them as if they don't have a fear of fighting is treating women the same way he or she would treat a man.

McCaughey theorizes that "by infiltrating an arena that has enabled men to solidify a naturalized sense of raw and physical masculine power, women cease to be merely fought-over objects, pretty property, or the ones behind the scenes nursing the male warriors." (178)

Some feminists disagree, of course, saying that women are buying into the dominant culture. What is obvious is that women in contact sports, by enjoying that which is aggressive and physical, threaten the association of masculinity with physical aggression. "Can we, should we, actually enjoy mock combat?" McCaughey asks. (144) The answer of women in contact sports is a resounding, "Yes!" And as feminists, we need to understand that women in contact sports aren't necessarily "dupes" of a patriarchal system. Instead, they are exploring what it means to be a woman—they are defining for themselves what it means to be a woman. And let's not forget that women are entitled to make their own choices, even if we might disagree with them. To argue otherwise is to reduce women to the status of infants and children, incapable of making legitimate choices, unable to act in their own best interest. That kind of paternalism is exactly what disturbs many of these athletes about what they conceive of as feminism.

Other implications are not so abstract as how (or if ) feminism should accommodate women's participation in contact sports. On a more mundane level, coaches report, "The new opportunities are accompanied by new pressures. Girls, their parents and fans are developing some of the same bad attitudes notorious in boys' sports." ("Growing Pains") What this means, according to Holly Gera, the athletic director at Montclair State University, "is that women respond like men to the same athletic pressures." ("Growing Pains") Probably, as women get more involved in sports, including contact sports, and as more opportunities open up, they will act more like men do. This can be both good and bad, but there shouldn't be a misguided belief that women in sports are somehow, for some reason, going to behave better than men in sports do.

A hockey player clarifies this issue: "I obviously believe in gender equity. But I don't think 'equity' means 'everything equal or exactly the same.' I don't want to see women blindly take the same paths as men and have the same downfalls." (Hallada-Pinhey)

This concern is important since we tend to perceive of female athletes as somehow less vulnerable than men to the excesses of sport. One hockey player says, "I think we can use the [1998] Winter Olympics as an example of the differences between women's and men's hockey. The [American] women won gold and went home successful and happy. The men lost after going into the competitions too confident, and trashed their hotel rooms afterwards. Who was the better sport?" (Wellman) The question, of course, is how long will this distinction last?

Throughout history, women have tried to create a space for female athletes, using a different model than the male model that dominates. But attempts to form a female model of sport have been unsuccessful and disappointing, even to some degree damaging as female leaders have prevented women from competing in an attempt to keep them from following the male model. (Cahn 76)

For many years, leaders of women's sports artificially discouraged competition, not allowing women to compete in varsity sports, refusing to allow women to play against each other in games. Many reasons existed for this, often linked to the fear that competition could injure women, and to the idea that competition in any event was "unwomanly." Instead, women were encouraged to view sports as recreation, as something they could do with their male partners and family members, like a social game of tennis.

Not surprisingly, this infuriates many female athletes who feel that feminists and female sports leaders don't "get it." These athletes feel feminist theorists are out of touch with the realities of their lives, and feminism is seen as ineffectual, whereas learning how to punch someone seems more relevant and useful. Others feel that their involvement in contact sports breaks down barriers far more than feminist theorizing does; many of these women accuse feminist theorists of preserving the status quo, of seeing women as victims, not as change agents in their own right; they see feminists as assuming masculine and feminine qualities are biological and not culturally imposed. Although they may not have the sophisticated language to express their thoughts in the way that scholars do, many female athletes have reached the conclusion that there is less difference between men and women than people are willing to acknowledge, and most simply wish to be left alone to pursue their goals and dreams without having to defend goals that men would never be asked to defend.

McCaughey puts it thus: "We might say that women are not so much devoted to appearing womanly as they are to allowing greater room for what can count culturally as 'womanly.'" (138) A football player agrees. "Women in contact sports can only be a good thing. They act as role models and expand the possibilities for all women." (Noah)

Female sports leaders point out that there must be an alternate model to the one currently in place, which consists of crass commercialism, corruption and an obsession with winning. The male model, they claim, is fundamentally sexist, elitist and exploitive. (Cahn 247) A football player agrees that changes in sports culture need to be made but remarks that "this is *not* only women's responsibility." (Noah)

We should contain our destructive urges, some say, rather than unleash them. One women relates the story of a friend who is a member of a fundamentalist Christian group that values complete non-violence and passivity. "She [the religious friend] mentioned today about one member who has been criticized because his son plays football. It then occurred to me that martial arts would be looked down on. It was shocking in a way to realize that because most people I know are supportive. ... I guess this perspective is just completely foreign to me" (Stambaugh).

One boxer, at least, doesn't worry about whether women should play sports differently from men. Professional boxer Jacqui Frazier-Lyde, speaking to a reporter about the possibility of a boxing match with Laila Ali, says, "it would be a great draw. It would establish Laila financially, and then I would establish her horizontally," displaying the braggadoccio common to male boxers. ("Familiar Names")

This is in line with research done that shows coaches and athletes believing that as more and more women participate in sports and as more and more opportunities open for them, they begin to follow the male model and act as male athletes do. In some cases, this might be good, in other cases, not so positive.

The Women's Sports Foundation has funded studies about the needs of professional and amateur female athletes, setting out areas that need to be addressed, such as ensuring equal funding and compensation for women's sports and female athletes, the establishment of athletes' advisory committees, support for hiring female coaches, encouraging the involvement of former athletes, establishment of players' associations, and more. The Foundation states that women's sports and women athletes continue to be underfunded, that communication between athletes and their sports' governing bodies must be improved, gender inequity continues to be a problem despite media hype, women athletes and women sports do not receive adequate publicity and promotion, more female coaches are needed, and greater representation by women is needed in governing organizations. (Women's Sports Foundation, 2 - 3)

Other organizations express similar goals. The International Female Boxers Association (IFBA) reports

*One of the primary goals of the IFBA is to develop female boxing into a sport which will persuade Olympic committees that women's boxing is worthy of being included in future world games as well as gathering support for the*

*future induction of women in the Boxing Hall of Fame.* (International Female Boxers Association website)

These worthy goals are not helped by societal emphasis on the attractiveness of female athletes as the most important measure of "feminine" success. For example, *The Black Book*, a resource directory for martial artist and martial arts instructors, routinely profiles female martial artists in its pages. Women interested in being profiled are required to submit a photo of themselves in a bikini. Obviously, such ridiculous requirements will end when women stop sending in pictures of themselves in bikinis.

In early 2001, *Playboy* sponsored a "Choose America's Sexiest Sportscaster Contest" and they weren't talking about Bob Costas. *Playboy's* website asked male readers to vote on the "hottest" of 10 female television sportscasters. "The winner will be asked to pose nude in an upcoming issue," the magazine's sports editor said. A *Sports Illustrated* reporter comments, "A poll such as *Plaboy's* only contributes to the difficulty in distinguishing which females on television are pursuing sports journalism and which are merely pursuing stardom"—as if any of the women had chosen to participate in the contest.

Fox Sports Net's Jeanne Zelasko says, "We're backsliding. When I talk to young women about careers in the field, do I advise them to get a solid background in sports and reporting, or do I tell them to enter a beauty contest?" ("Hottie Topic")

Despite these frustrations, many women believe that women in sports—and women in contact sports—can create a new model of what sports can be like. Former pro basketball player and sportswriter Mariah Burton Nelson posits a "partnership" approach that emphasizes viewing one another as "comrades" rather than enemies. (9) She says, "Players with disparate ability levels are respected as peers rather than ranked in a hierarchy and athletes care for each other and their own bodies." (9) She insists that this view is not anti-competitive (a complaint often leveled against female sports models) and that friendly rivalries would still exist. (10) Power, she goes on to say, "is understood not as power-over (power as dominance) but power-to (power as competence)." (9)

The biggest hurdle to a more female-friendly sports model is that men control women's sports. Women in sports, especially contact sports, have mostly male coaches. There are reasons for this, many of them having to do with organizations like the NCAA muscling out women's leadership of women's sports, but mostly because only recently have large numbers of women participated in violent sports. Men can coach women but women rarely coach men; if a woman enjoyed playing ice hockey as a teenager, she never envisioned herself as a coach. There just weren't enough opportunities.

There are numerous problems with male-dominance of women's sports. One of these problems is the abuse of female athletes by male coaches.

A martial artist describes her encounters with her male instructor:

*He asked me out, and I turned him down. (I was 16 years old and he was in his 20s). It cost me a miserable training session and many, many push-ups in front of everyone else. Another time ... I declined ... and was forced to spar only with him. He kick the sh— out of me. Nothing like being stupid, determined and finally persevering! I was the first and only woman in my dojo* [training hall]. *Often we had to spar on a balance beam ... My instructor once grabbed my jacket* [uniform top] *... and ripped it down the front... I stayed on the balance beam as he fell. It was about then I decided that I should wear a shirt under my jacket.* (Bunker)

Yet a rugby player shares a different experience of her male coach, who occasionally scrimmages with the all-female team:

*He's great to play against because his tackles are perfect. He could really really hurt us (he's a big guy), but he's very careful to set us down rather than knock us down. I know he's not playing at full capacity with us but that's ok. He's bigger, stronger, faster and has more skill than most of the team.* (Womack)

In college women's sports, "it's male coaches who are coming and females who are going," according to a recent article in *Sports Illustrated for Women*. (Anderson, K., 88) 80% of all head coaching jobs (for women's teams) have gone to men. In 1972, when Title IX was enacted, 90% of women's teams had female head coaches.

Sportswriter Mariah Burton Nelson says simply, "Name one outstanding female athlete and chances are she has a male coach" (158). In contact sports, amateur and recreation-level female athletes almost always have male coaches.

"It does not make sense," says Barbara Hedges, the athletic director of the University of Washington. (Anderson, K., 88) The stakes have gotten higher, with higher salaries, more scholarships, television contracts and more. Mary Jo Kane, director of the Tucker Center for Research on Girls and Women in Sport at the University of Minnesota, says, "There is still a deep-seated cultural assumption that if you want to take your program to the big time, you want to get a *real* coach, so you should get a male coach." (Anderson, K., 88)

The University of Iowa's athletic director, Christine Grant speculates: "I don't think there is a concerted effort to go and get qualified women. ... Male athletic directors apparently aren't doing that. When they hire their male coaches, they are on the phone with buddies finding out what their recommendations are. It's an entirely different method of recruitment." (Anderson, K., 88)

Others say women have not had the opportunity to gain the knowledge and experience necessary to become head coaches. In addition, many programs are combined—one head coach coaches both men's and women's volleyball, for instance. Men almost always get these jobs for two reasons: men traditionally coach men's teams and men have more experience coaching than women do. (Anderson, K., 89) Sportswriter Nelson summarizes the varying perspectives this way: women blame the old boy network and men blame the lack of qualified women. (166)

Further complicating matters, some eligible women have no desire to be head coaches, citing extensive travel, pressure and time commitments that conflict with a balanced family life and other responsibilities. (Anderson, K., 89 - 90) Single female coaches, who might be willing to take on the job are perceived as lesbians and recruited against that way. (Anderson, K., 91)

A hockey coach says, "I had intended to coach 'hockey' not 'girls' hockey' or 'boys' hockey' but I found ... that volunteers were badly needed and that though dads would sign up to coach their sons' teams, no one was willing to commit to starting and coaching a girls' team. This seemed goofy to me so I stepped forward." (McDowell) Education is of great importance, Coach McDowell says. "It is often the mom that says to her daughter, 'Oh, honey, you don't want to do that' or 'We'd love to have our daughter play but we're so busy taking our son to x, y, z, that we just don't have time.'" She goes on to say, "We need more women participating in leadership roles—either as coaches, league administrators, rink owners, etc. *Otherwise, we're always just paying for the privilege of playing someone else's game.*" (McDowell) (italics mine)

Most of the female athletes interviewed for this book feel that more needs to be done to allow access to sports opportunities. Women in college sports express skepticism about the amount of progress that is being seen. At her school, one college athlete claims, the ratio of men to women in sports is about 5:1. "I know the laws exist, but they're not being upheld." (Wellman) One martial artist who played college sports points out that equipment and facilities for women are second rate compared to those given to men, and that women pay for a lot of expenses out of their own pockets. She says dryly, "If colleges can pay for men's jock straps, they ought to be able to pay for women's sports bras." (Dumin)

"I think a lot more needs to be done," says a rugby player. "Young girls should be encouraged to play outdoors, to play backyard games, climb trees. ... I am who I am because my parents allowed me to play with the boys, get dirty and be athletic. I never remember being encouraged to play sports in school. I was encouraged to do cheerleading ... but never to try softball" (Fancy).

A hockey player says:

*We have a very successful men's Division I team* [at her university] *that has their own locker room facilities.* [They] *practice in the middle of the afternoon while we, the women's team, are deprived of our varsity status* [even though] *we have proven to be worthy ... because we do not have a locker room* [therefore the NCAA won't allow them to play as a varsity team]. *We all show up at the rink at 5:30 a.m. to hit the ice at 6 a.m. We keep our equipment in the trunk of our cars to freeze in the winter, and we start most of our games at 10:30 p.m. All we are asking for is a locker room of our own.* (Ward)

Another woman says:

*Girls have been told for years that they can't play football, basketball, hockey, that they can't wrestle or pole vault. And dumbly, we believed them. For years growing up, mom and dad told me I couldn't mow the lawn, that that was a boy's*

*job, and that dishes and laundry were my jobs. It's the same concept. Now that I've been out on my own, I've discovered how much I love to mow the lawn. I just think our girls need to be given the chance ... It's up to my generation and the [younger] generations to prevent this sexist attitude from surviving. I want my daughters to have every chance possible to make their lives ... fulfilling ... and if that means donning hockey shorts or a wrestling singlet, I'm all for it.*
(Wellman)

One hockey players says, "I often wonder, 'What if I'd had the opportunity as a child—if I'd grown up playing organized hockey?' I'd be as good as the men. I've played softball since I was 6, and I can still hang with the guys. ... In sports, speed and agility can trade off with weight and size." In other words, women have attributes that can help them succeed when competing with men: they just need to have lifelong experience in sports like many men do. She goes on to say, "There are women in more advanced leagues who'd kill the guys in my league." (Lentz)

"There were few opportunities for girls when I was growing up," says a martial artist. "In high school, there was no basketball, no track, no volleyball—just skiing and only the elite skiers could compete. Sports should be available for everyone, even people who aren't elite and aren't going to be." (Anderson, V.)

One hockey player flatly states

*There is nothing even approaching gender equity in sports ... Comments about women's sports are often dictated by the attractiveness of the athlete (Gabrielle Reese) or the removal of a shirt. ... In high school, middle school and college the focus is on men's/boy's sports. Girls are second ... I think that sports are the very best defense for young women against drugs, bad men, anorexia, low self-esteem. ...Girls have spentso long being discouraged athletically that they need to be actively encouraged to achieve equity."*(Kangas, P.)

One hockey player whose background is in equestrian sports says, "What I grew up with, riding horses, was an interesting mix. Most of the young people who ride are female, most of the professionals at the adult level are men. I never figured it out." She goes on to say:

*Strong programs for girls [are] important ... Having the ability to participate in boys' programs is important, too, where there aren't enough girls to field a team or there isn't a high enough level of competition ... Coaches and game officials can send a big positive message to girls ... that girls' sports are just as important as boys' sports. And I think it's important for kids to see their moms and aunts and grand-mothers participate in sports—and not just traditionally female sports ... Oh, and one more thing—someplace to change your clothes when you're playing with men.* (Torrance)

A wrestling coach says, "There are no girls' teams in this state. Most girls don't want to wrestle boys. If there were girls' teams, there would be more girl wrestlers. In other states, they have very successful girls' wrestling programs." (Anderson, B.)

A hockey player says:

*League organizers consider themselves in compliance with gender equity since opportunities are now open to women players. They still do very little to make the playing condi-tions better for the women who choose to continue playing in the men's league (locker room, shower facilities, general acceptance).* [Few women are at her competitive level] *So I either give up competition with men or suffer lack of camaraderie, general acceptance and facilities playing with the men* (Hallada-Pinhey).

A football players says, "When I was in high school, I had to play on the men's soccer team because we did not have a women's team." She believes this has changed. "I think if there is a group of people, men or women, with a common interest, then they will find a way to play." She adds, a little sadly, "I would love to see equal pay for women in professional sports. I think this is a long time coming. Maybe someday." (Walsh) A football player points out the difference between men's and women's sports this way: "You'd never ask if men in a pro league were getting paid." (Noah) A rugby player laments that her team is financially dependent on the men's league that oversees it. She calls the relationship paternalistic and likens it to a bad marriage. Women's teams need separate and independent funding, she maintains. (Keyt)

One hockey player says, "We shouldn't overlook involving adult women in sports. It is so important for adults to try new sports. There's none of the nonsense of children's or young adults' leagues." (Schimanski-Gross)

Women in contact sports have the capacity to challenge and change what we think about what women can do and what women should do. A hockey player says, "I was better than the other goalies in the [men's] leagues. This amazed most of them. It opened up a lot of dialogue." (McDowell)

The truth is, whether we agree or disagree, there's no stopping them now. And most would say, the more pressing question is not why women participate in violent sports, but why they don't.

# Appendix

## TITLE IX, Education Amendments of 1972
## (Title 20 U.S.C. Sections 1681-1688)

Section 1681. Sex

(a) Prohibition against discrimination; exceptions. No person in the United States shall, on the basis of sex, be excluded from participation in, be denied the benefits of, or be subjected to discrimination under any education program or activity receiving Federal financial assistance, except that:

(1) Classes of educational institutions subject to prohibition in regard to admissions to educational institutions, this section shall apply only to instutiions of vocational education, professional education and graduate higher education, and to public institutions of undergraduate higher education;

(2) Educational in regard to admission to educational institutions, this section shall not apply (A) for one year from June 23, 1972, nor for six years after June 23, 1972, in the case of an educational institution which has begun the process of changing from being an institution which admits only students of

one sex to being an institution which admits students of both sexes, but only if it is carrying out a plan for such a change which is approved by the Secretary of Education or (B) for seven years from the date an educational institution begins the process of changing from being an institution which admits only students of one sex to being an institution which admits students of both sexes, but only if it is carrying out a plan for such a change which is approved by the Secretary of Education, whichever is later;

(3) Educational institutions of religious organizations with contrary religious tenets this section shall not apply to any educational institution which is controlled by a religious organization if the application of this subsection would not be consistent with the religious tenets of such organization;

(4) Educational institutions training individuals for military service or merchant marine this section shall not apply to an educational institution whose primary purpose is the training of individuals for the military services of the United States or the merchant marine;

(5) Public educational institutions with traditional and continuing admissions policyin regard to admissions this section shall not apply to any public institution of undergraduate higher education which is an institution that traditionally and continually from its establishment has had a policy of admitting only students of one sex;

(6) Social fraternities or sororities; voluntary youth service organizations this section shall not apply to membership practices —

(A) of a social fraternity or social sorority which is exempt from taxation under section 501 (a) of Title 26, the active membership of which consists primarily of students in attendance at an institution of higher education, or

(B) of the Young Men's Christian Association, Young Women's Christian Association; Girl Scouts; Boy Scouts; Camp Fire Girls, and voluntary youth service organizations which are so exempt, the membership of which has traditionally been limited to persons of one sex and principally to persons less than 19 years of age;

(7) Boy or Girl Conferences
this section shall not apply to —

(A) any program or activity of the American Legion undertaken in connection with the organization or operation of any Boys State conference, Boys Nation conference, Girls State conference, or Girls Nation conference; or

(B) any program or activity of any secondary school or educational institution specifically for —
(i) the promotion of any Boys State conference, Boys Nation conference, Girls State conference, or Girls Nation conference; or
(ii) the selection of students to attend any such conference;

8) Father-son or mother-daughter activities at educational institutions. This section shall not preclude father-son or mother-daughter activities at an educational institution, but if such activities are provided for students of one sex, opportunities for reasonably comparable activities shall be provided for students of the other sex; and

(9) Institutions of higher education scholarship awards in "beauty" pageants this section shall not apply with respect to any scholarship or other financial assistance awarded by an institution of higher education to any individual because such individual has received such award in any pageant in which the attainment of such award is based upon a combination of factors related to the personal appearance, poise, and talent of such individual and in which participation is limited to individuals of one sex only, so long as the pageant is in compliance with other nondiscrimination provisions of Federal law.

(b) Preferential or disparate treatment because of imbalance in participation or receipt of Federal benefits; statistical evidence of imbalance.

Nothing contained in subsection (a) of this section shall be interpreted to require any educational institution to grant preferential or disparate treatment to the members of one sex on account of an imbalance which may exist with respect to the total number or percentage of persons of that sex participating in or receiving the benefits of any federally supported program or acticity, in comparison with the total number or percentage of persons of that sex in any community, State, section, or other area: *Provided*, that this subsection shall not be construed to prevent the consideration in any hearing or proceeding under this chapter of statistical evidence tending to show that such an imbalance exists with respect to the participation in, or receipt of the benefits of, any such program or activity by members of one sex.

(c) Educational institution defined.
For the purposes of this chapter an educational institution means any public or private preschool, elementary, or second-

ary school, or any institution of vocational, professional or higher education, except that in the case of an educational institution composed of more than one school, college, or department which are administratively separate units, such term means each such school, college or deaprtment.

Section 1682. Federal administrative enforcement; report to Congressional comitteees

Each Federal department and agency which is empowered to extend Federal financial assistance to any educational program or activity, by way of grant, loan, or contract other than a contract of insurance or guaranty, is authorized and directed to effectuate the provisions of section 1681 of this title with respect to such program or activity by issuing rules, regulations, or order of general applicability which shall be consistent with achievement of the objectives of the statute authorizing the financial assistance in connection with which the action is taken. No such rule, regulation, or order shall become effective unless and until approved by the President. Compliance with any requirement adopted pursuant to this section may be effected (1) by the termination of or refusal to grant or to continue assistance under such program or activity to any recipient as to whom there has been an express finding on the record, after opportunity for hearing, of a failure to comply with such requirement, but such termination or refusal shall be limited to the particular political entity, or part thereof, or other recipient as to whom such a finding has been made, and shall be limited in it effect to the particular program, or part thereof, in which such noncompliance has been found, or (2) by any other means authorized by law: *Provided, however,* that no such action shall be taken until the department or agency concerned has advised the appropriate person or persons of the failure to comply with the requirement and has determined that compliance cannot be secured by voluntary means. In the case of any action terminating, or refusing to grant or continue, assistance because of failure to comply with a requirement imposed pursuant to this section, the head of the Federal department or agency shall file with the committees of the House and Senate having legislative jurisdiction over the program or activity involved a full written report of the circumstances and the grounds for such action. No such action shall become effective until thirty days have elapsed after the filing of such report.

Section 1683. Judicial Review

Any department or agency action taken pursuant to section 1682 of this title shall be subject to such judicial review as may otherwise be provided by law for similar action taken by such department or agency on other grounds. In the case of action, not otherwise subject to judicial review, terminating or refusing to grant or to continue financial assistance upon a finding of failure to comply with any requirement imposed pursuant to section 1682 of this title, any person aggrieved (incluidng any State or political subdivision thereof and any agency of either) may obtain judicial review of such action in accordance with chapter 7 of title 5, United States Code, and such action shall not be deemed committed to unreviewable agency discretion within the meaning of section 701 of that title.

Section 1684. Blindness or visual impairment; prohibition against discrimination

No person in the United States shall, on the ground of blindness or severely impaired vision, be denied admission in any course of study by a recipient of Federal financial assistance for any education program or activity; but nothing herein shall be construed to require any such institution to provide any special services to such person because of his blindness or visual impairement.

Section 1685. Authority under other laws unaffected

Nothing in this chapter shall add to or detract from any existing authority with respect to any program or activity under which Federal financial assistance is extended by way of a contract of insurance or guaranty.

Section 1686. Interpretation with respect to living facilities

Nothwithstanding anything to the contrary contained in this chapter, nothing contained herein shall be construed to prohibit any educational institution receiving funds under this Act, from maintaining separate living facilities for the different sexes.

Section 1687. Interpretation of "program or activity"

For this purposes of this title the term "program or activity" and "program" mean all of the operations of —

(1)(A) a department, agency, special purpose district, or other instrumentality of a State or of a local government; or

(B) the entity of such State or local government that distributed such assistance and each such department or agency (and each other State or local government entity) to which the assistance is extended, in the case of assistance to a State or local government;

(2)(A) a college, university, or other postsecondary institution or public system of higher education; or

(B) a local educational agency . . .system of vocational education, or other school system;

(3)(A) an entire corporation, partnership or other private organization or an entire sole proprietorship —

(i) if assistance is extended to such corporation, partnership, private organization or sole proprietorship as a whole; or

(ii) which is principally engaged in the business of providing education, health care, housing, social services, or parks and recreation; or

(B) the entire plant or other comparable, geographically separate facility to which Federal financial assistance is extended, in the case of any other corporatioin, partnership, private organization, or sole proprietorship; or

(4) any other entity which is established by two or more of the entities described in paragraph (1), (2) or (3);

any part of which is extended Federal financial assistance, except that such term does not include any operation of an entity which is controlled by a religious organization if the application of section 1681 of this title to such operation would not be consistent with the religious tenets of such organization.

Section 1688. Neutrality with respect to abortion

Nothing in this chapter shall be construed to require or prohibit any person or public or private entity, to provide or pay for any benefit or service, including the use of facilities, related to an abortion. Nothing in this section shall be construed to permit a penalty to be imposed on any person or individual because such person or individual is seeking or has received any benefit or service related to a legal abortion.

# The Brighton Declaration (1994)

## A. SCOPE AND AIMS OF THE DECLARATION

### 1. SCOPE

This declaration is addressed to all those governments, public authorities, organisations, businesses, educational and research establishments, women's organisations and individuals who are responsible for, or who directly or indirectly influence, the conduct, development or promotion of sport or who are in any way involved in the employment, education, management, training, development or care of women in sport. This Declaration is meant to complement all sporting, local, national and international charters, laws, codes, rules and regulations relating to women or sport.

### 2. AIMS

The overriding aim is to develop a sporting culture that enables and values the involvement of women in every aspect of sport.

It is in the interests of equality, development and peace that a commitment be made by governmental, non-governmental organisations and those institutions involved in sport to apply the Principles set out in this Declaration by developing appropriate policies, structures and mechanisms which:

- ensure that all women and girls have opportunity to participate in sport in a safe and supportive environment which preserves the rights, dignity and respect of the individual;
- increase the involvement of women in sport at all levels and in all functions and roles;
- ensure that the knowledge, experiences and values of women contribute to the development of sport;

- promote the recognition of women's involvement in sport as a contribution to public life, community development and in building a healthy nation;
- promote the recognition by women of the intrinsic value of sport and its contribution to personal development and healthy lifestyle.

## B. THE PRINCIPLES
## 1. EQUITY AND EQUALITY IN SOCIETY AND SPORT

a. Every effort should be made by state and government machineries to ensure that institutions and organisations responsible for sport comply with the equality provisions of the Charter of the United Nations, the Universal Declaration of Human Rights and the UN Convention on the Elimination of All Forms of Discrimination against Women.

b. Equal opportunity to participate and be involved in sport whether for the purpose of leisure and recreation, health promotion or high performance, is the right of every woman, regardless of race, colour, language, religion, creed, sexual orientation, age, marital status, disability, political belief or affliation, national or social origin.

c. Resources, power and responsibility should be allocated fairly and without discrimination on the basis of sex, but such allocation should redress any inequitable balance in the benefits available to men and women.

## 2. FACILITIES
Women's participation in sport is influenced by the extent, variety and accessibility of facilities. The planning, design and management of these should appropriately and equitably meet the particular needs of women in the community, with special

attention given to the need for child care provision and safety.

## 3. SCHOOL AND JUNIOR SPORT

Research demonstrates that girls and boys approach sports from markedly different perspectives. Those responsible for sport, education, recreation and physical education of young people should ensure that an equitable range of opportunities and learning exerpeince, which accommodate the values, attitudes and aspirations of girls, is incorporated in programmes to develop physical fitness and basic sport skills of young people.

## 4. DEVELOPING PARTICIPATION

Women's participation in sport is influenced by the range of activities available. Those responsible for delivering sporting opportunities and programmes should provide and promote activities which meet women's needs and aspirations.

## 5. HIGH PERFORMANCE SPORT

a. Governments and sports organisations should provide equal opportunities to women to reach their sports performance potential by ensuring that all activities and programmes relating to performance improvements take account of the specific needs of female athletes.

b. Those supporting elite and/or professional athletes should ensure that competition opportunities, rewards, incentives, recognition, sponsorship, promotion and other forms of support are provided fairly and equitably to both women and men.

## 6. LEADERSHIP IN SPORT

Women are under-represented in the leadership and decision making of all sport and sport-related organisations. Those responsible for these areas should develop policies and programmes and design structures which increase the number of women coaches, advisers, decision makers, officials, administrators and sports personnel at all levels with special attention given to recruitment, development and retention.

## 7. EDUCATION, TRAINING AND DEVELOPMENT
Those responsible for the education, training and development of coaches and other sports personnel should ensure that education processes and experiences address issues relating to gender equity and the needs of female athletes, equitably reflect women's role in sport and take account of women's leadership experiences, values and attitudes.

## 8. SPORT INFORMATION AND RESEARCH
Those responsible for research and providing information on sport should develop policies and programmes to increase knowledge and understanding about women and sport and ensure that research norms and standards are based on research on women and men.

## 9. RESOURCES
Those responsible for the allocation of resources should ensure that support is available for sportswomen, women's programmes, and special measures to advance this Declaration of Principles.

## 10. DOMESTIC AND INTERNATIONAL COOPERATION
Government and non-government organisations should incorporate the promotion of issues of gender equity and the sahring of examples of good practice in women and sport policies and programmes in their associations with other organisations within both domestic and international arenas.

# The Windhoek Conference Call for Action

In addition to re-affirming the principles of the Brighton Declaration, the delegates called for action in the following areas:

1. Develop action plans with objectives and targets to implement principles of the Brighton Declaration, and monitor and report upon their implementation.

2. Reach out beyond the current boundaries of the sport sector to the global women's equality movement and develop closer partnerships between sport and women's organisations on the one side, and representatives from sectors such as education, youth, health, human rights and employment on the other. Develop strategies that help other sectors obtain their objectives through the medium of sport and at the same time further sport objectives.

3. Promote and share information about the positive contribution that girls' and women's involvement in sport makes, inter alia, to social, health and economic issues.

4. Build the capacity of women as leaders and decision-makers and ensure that women play meaningful and visible roles in sport at all levels. Create mechanisms that ensure that young women have a voice in the development of policies and programmes that affect them.

5. Avert the 'world crisis in physical education' by establishing and strengthening quality physical education programmes as key means for the positive introduction to young girls of the

skills and other benefits they can acquire through sport. Further, create policies and mechanisms that ensure progression from sport to community-based activity.

6. Encourage the media to positively portray and significantly cover the breadth, depth, quality, and benefits of girls' and women's involvement in sports.

7. Ensure a safe and supportive environment for girls and women participating in sport at all levels by taking steps to eliminate all forms of harassment and abuse, violence and exploitation, and gender testing.

8. Ensure that policies and programmes provide opportunities for all girls and women in full recognition of the differences and diversity among them—including such factors as race, ability, age, religion, sexual orientation, ethnicity, language, culture or their status as an indigenous person.

9. Recognise the importance of governments to sports development and urge them to conduct gender impact analyses and to develop appropriate legislation, public policy and funding that ensures gender equality in all aspects of sport.

10. Ensure that Official Development Assistance programmes provide equal opportunities for girls' and women's development and recognise the potential of sport to achieve development objectives.

11. Encourage more women to become researchers in sport, and more research to be undertaken on critical issues relating to women in sport.

# *Our Ice Rink*
## Suzanne Schimanski-Gross
(Copyright © 2001 Suzanne Schimanski-Gross)

*I wrote the following story about my family's ice rink in 1985.
You will read about my brothers. One died suddenly, of myocarditis, in March 1975. That was Steve, the oldest (5 years older than
me). He taught me how to skate backward. The gentle slope in our
backyard helped, too.*

*My second oldest brother Paul died suddenly in a car accident
in 1999. He was my one brother who was still playing hockey when
I began. He played on two teams and had some extra equipment he
loaned me. After he died, one of his teams had his number, 55, added
to the shoulders of their jerseys. I and two of my teammates did
this, too.*

*Playing hockey brings me closer to my brothers. I like to think a
little of their spirit lives on and plays hockey with me. I have two
living brothers, Mike and John. They are three years older than me.
They and my parents are pretty proud of me playing. Paul was
proud of me, too. He only saw a video of me playing and wondered
why we all appeared to be standing still. It was our first season, and
we were SLOW. We were all really new at it.*

*I hope you like the story.*

As the snow fluttered down from the clouds, images of winters past drifted through my mind. I recalled the winters of my childhood. Is the snow accumulating yet? As soon as we get an inch or two, we can start making the ice rink. After a few days with false hopes, the snow stayed and we began flattening the snow in our backyard. We took the big red sleds from their nail on the wall of the garage. I climbed in one and cinder blocks filled the other. To compress the snow, my brothers pulled the sleds over the snow in the same striped pattern in which they mowed the lawn. To pack it even tighter, we trampled over our sled trails, and soon our backyard looked like the surface of the moon with our footprints as the craters.

When my dad came home from work, we hauled the garden hose from the garage and hooked it to the spigot on the back of the house. Using a spray nozzle, my dad flooded the yard of craters with water, which froze quickly in the Muskegon air. After he applied a few coats, we stomped on the crunchy, crusty ice to make it smoother and break any air holes for the second watering. We repeated these steps over a period of hours or days, depending on how cold it was, until our backyard was covered by a uniformly smooth sheet of ice which stretched lengthwise from the brick fortress fence on the left to the chain link on the right and widthwise from the back porch to the beginning of Mrs. Williams' backyard.

The borders of the rink began in the irregular pattern of a jigsaw puzzle piece, but as the weeks passed by, snow banks grew to frame the rink. These banks were our "boards." They were much softer to smash into than the wooden ones at the L.C. Walker Ice Arena. The banks served as a resting area for weary skaters and also held hockey sticks, snow shovels and discarded hats and mittens.

Our rink was of fair size, but my parents saw no need to purchase a Zamboni to resurface the ice. Instead we relied upon a system whose main element was people. Every time snow fell, we pulled the shovels from the banks and pushed them across the ice, working with halves or quarters or even smaller sections depending upon the weight of the snow. When the snow was light and fluffy, shoveling was an easy task. The snow would almost jump into the bank, using the momentum of the skater behind it. When the snow was slushy and dense, it took an eternity to shovel. I could heave only a few shovels full before I fell exhausted into the snow bank to rest.

As I lay on the mound of snow, I stared up at the black evening sky. The snow pelted down at my face, making it difficult to discern between the crystalline flakes and the constellations. I had to be careful not to stare too long to avoid getting dizzy. After I regained my strength, I resumed clearing the ice with my brothers.

With the shoveling complete, it was time for me to go to bed and for my brothers to begin their watering shifts. Each took a turn flooding the rink. After their shifts were through, our dad began his nightly ritual. Using the garden hose, he flooded the ice several times. He was out there till midnight to ensure we had a smooth surface to skate on the next day.

Each morning as I looked out the kitchen window, I saw a blanket of newly fallen or drifted snow covering our previous ice. When neighbor kids came over to play hockey we all labored to clear the ice. Then my brothers placed the goals at their respective ends of the rink. These goals, made with steel piping and nylon netting, were designed and custom built by our dad. My brothers and their friends divided themselves into teams and dropped the puck. As the screams and shouts and cheers of excitement grew louder, more kids were attracted to the fun. Occasionally older boys from outside the neighborhood joined the game. Our mom asked them to leave because they would try to kick my brothers and me off our own rink.

My friends also came to skate. We usually ended up in a corner, away from the action and on bumpy ice. My only chance to develop my stick handling techniques came when there were not enough players and I got to play until more guys came, or when my brothers let me be all-time goalie. Sometimes we designated a time for just skating and allowed no pucks or sticks on the rink. Skaters of all kinds were there: figure skaters, speed skaters, little kids with double runners, adults who were just learning by supporting themselves with chairs, and of course, showoffs. As it grew darker, the crowd changed but still remained. The time would come to turn on our spotlights. Two high power spotlights were mounted on a board placed in my parents' bedroom window, located on the left side of the second story. The most spectacular light of all stood solitary in the center of the rear border of our backyard. High on a post as tall as a street light, perched three more spotlights. Together, these lights brightened our backyard as if it were day.

We skated day and night, pausing only to warm our toes and fingers to revive them from numbness. We dedicated every minute of our winter fun to the ice rink in our backyard. Everything else in the world stopped, and our ice rink was the center of activity. Then the sun shone longer and brighter, and the snow did not fall as frequently. The ice became slushy and mushy at times and we could not always skate during the day or afternoon and had to wait until evening when the temperature would drop enough to refreeze our ice. Patches of grass broke through the ice, but we could still skate on parts of it. We would get a light snowfall, but then the sun would come again and dash our hopes. Now each morning as I looked out the window, I saw our ice rink dissolving into a grassy swamp. Only fractions of crusty snow banks remained to support a few fallen shovels and hockey sticks.

# Works Cited

"About the WSF." Women's Sports Foundation website. Online: www.wsf.org.uk/about.htm.

Albright, Andrea, "Football Camp Focuses on Girls." *Topeka Capital-Journal*. Online: cjonline.com.

Anderson, Brian "Chip." Telephone interview. January 25, 2001.

Anderson, Chantal. Telephone interview. January 25, 2001.

Anderson, Kelli, "Where Are all the Women Coaches," *Sports Illustrated for Women* (Jan/Feb 201): 87 - 91.

Anderson, Vickie. Telephone interview. January 25, 2001.

"Another Ali: Muhammad's daughter to make boxing debut," CNN/SI. Online: www.si.com. October 14, 1999.

Bove, Susan. Personal letter. December 30, 2000.

Brighton Declaration, the. Online: www.iwg-gti.org/e/brighton/index.htm.

Bunker, Amy. Personal letters (e-mail). December 8 - 20, 2000.

Cahn, Susan K. *Coming On Strong: Gender and Sexuality in Twentieth-Century Women's Sport*. Cambridge: Harvard UP, 1994.

Carter, Ivan, "This Homecoming Princess has game on the football field," *Kansas City Star* (October 20, 2000). Online: www.kcstar.com.

Chrysler Viking Mermaids Ladies' American Football Club website. Online: www.viennavikings.com/mermaids/we.htm.

Covitz, Randy, "Rugby Attracts diverse group of KC area women and they're good at it," *Kansas City Star* (March 19, 2000) :C-15.

Cox, Johanna. Personal letter. November 4, 2000.

Dohrmann, George, "Running into Full Contact: Women's Football Debuts," *Real Sports* (Winter 1999): 24 -27.

——, "Girl Trouble," *Sports Illustrated* (January 8, 2001): 26.

Dowling, Colette. *The Frailty Myth: Women Approaching Physial Equality.* New York: Random House, 2000.

Dumin, JoAnn. Telephone interview. December 15, 2000.

Dutter, Suzanne. Chrysler Viking Mermaids Ladies' American Football Club website. Online: www.viennavikings.com/mermaids.

Eaden, Sheron. Personal letter. October 20, 2000.

"Falling in Line: Freeda Foreman Joins Boxing Daughters of Ali, Frazier," CNN/SI. Online: www.si.com. October 10, 2000.

"Familiar Names: Daughters of Ali and Frazier could meet in the ring," CNN/SI. Online: www.si.com. December 21, 1999.

Fancy, Ann. Personal letter. December 19, 2000.

Farber, Michael, "Her Body of Work," *Sports Illustrated for Women* (Jan/Feb 2001): 94 - 95.

Formosa, Patty. Personal letter (e-mail). January 28, 2001.

Friesen, Dena. Personal interview. November 9, 2000.

"Girls Football," *Toledo Blade* (September 5, 1978). Online: www.fortunecity.com/wembley/mueller/641.

Goudsmit, A. Poppy. Personal letter (e-mail). December 12, 2000.

Grabowski, Nadine. Personal letter (e-mail). December 14, 2000.

"Growing Pains: As female participation grows, so do problems," CNN/SI. Online: www.si.com. July 26, 1999.

Guttmann, Allen. *Women's Sports: A History*. New York: Columbia UP, 1991.

Hall, M. Ann. *Boxers and Body Makers: Third Wave Feminism and the Remaking of Women's Sport*. Canadian Association for the Advancement of Women and Sports (CAAWS) website. Online: www/caaws.ca/gender_equity/boxers-bodyb.htm. January 30, 2001.

Hallada-Pinhey, Kate. Personal letter (e-mail). January 28, 2001.

Heys, Patricia, "Week at a Glance: A Future Emerging for Females in Football," CNN/SI. Online: www.si.com. September 22, 2000.

"Hottie Topic,"*Sports Illustrated* (January 24, 2001): 22.

Infotelefon Female Football League website.

Online: www.ladiesfootball.de/english.

International Female Boxers Association (IFBA) website. Online: www.ifba.com.

International Working Group on Women and Sport website. Online: www.iwg-gti.org/e/about/index.htm.

Kangas, Greta. Personal letter (e-mail). February 5, 2001.

Kangas, Pam. Personal letter. January 10, 2001.

Kantor, Stuart. *The History of Women's Professional Football.* Online: www.women'sprofootball.com.

Keyt, Ellen. Telephone interview. December 18, 2000.

Lentz, Carol. Telephone interview. December 20, 2000.

Levy, Jaime, "Appeals Court Reinstates Duke Female Kicker's Title IX Suit," CNN/SI. Online: www.si.com. July 21, 1999.

"Mama Manon: Motherhood doesn't diminish Rheaume's pipe dreams," CNN/SI. Online: www.si.com. July 25, 1999.

"Man vs. Woman: Battle of the Sexes Reaches New Level Saturday," CNN/SI. Online: www.si.com. October 14, 1999.

McCaughey, Martha. *Real Knockouts: The Physical Feminism of Women's Self-Defense.* New York: New York UP, 1997.

McDowell, Sue. Personal letter (e-mail). December 20, 2000.

Menard, Louis, "Sporting Chances," *The New Yorker* (January 22, 2001): 84 - 88.

Monson, Michele. Personal letter (e-mail). January 20, 2001.

"Narrowing the Gap: NCAA Reports number of female athletes up to 40%," CNN/SI. Online: www.si.com. October 26, 2000.

National Women's Football League (NWFL) website. Online: www.angelfire.com/tn2/nwflcentral.

Nelson, Mariah Burton. *Are We Winning Yet? How Women Are Changing Sports and Sports Are Changing Women.* New York: Random House, 1991.

Noah, Laura. Telephone interview. December 16, 2000.

"Out of the Shadows: Foundation Still Fighting for Rights of Female Athletes," CNN/SI. Online: www.si.com. October 19, 1999.

Park, Shelley. Personal letter (e-mail). December 12, 2000.

Picket, Lynn Snowden. *Looking for a Fight: A Memoir*. New York: Random House, 2000.

Poehler, Kathy. Telephone interview. December 18, 2000.

Ransom, La Tricia, "Finding Power Within: Martial Arts Builds Strength of Spirit, " *Real Sports*(Winter 1999): 65 - 67.

Robinson, Lisa. Personal letter. October 25, 2000.

Schimanski-Gross, Suzanne. Personal letters (e-mail) and telephone interview. December 20, 2000 - February 15, 2001.

Sekules, Kate. *The Boxer's Heart: How I Fell in Love with the Ring*. New York: Villard, 2000.

Smith, Lissa, ed. *Nike is a Goddess: The History of Women in Sports*. New York: Atlantic Monthly Press, 1998.

Sportscotland website. Online: www.sportscotland.org.uk.

"Spotlight: Jean Martin, Boxer," CNN/SI. Online: www.si.com. April 5, 1999.

St. Jorre, John de, "The Next Ali, " *Women's Sports and Fitness* (July/August 2000): 110.

Stambaugh, Carol. Personal letter. October 25, 2000.

"Storm History." New England Storm website. Online: www.newenglandstorm.com.

"Sydney: 20 to Watch, " *Women's Sports + Fitness* (September 2000): 72.

Theberge, Nancy. *Higher Goals: Women's Ice Hockey and the Politics of Gender*. New York: State UP of New York P, 2000.

"This Frazier has another motivation," *Kansas City Star* (March 19, 2000): C-2.

Torrance, Megan. Personal letter (e-mail). January 7, 2000.

"Touchdown: High School Junior Joins Elite Company with Three-Yard Run," CNN/SI. Online: www.si.com. September 19, 1999.

Troutwine, Cheryl. Personal letter (e-mail). January 19, 2001.

"Two Girls Suit Up for Seqouyah Football Team" *The Shawnee News-Star* (September 26, 1999). Online: www.new-star.com.

Uzelac, Monique. Telephone interview. December 15, 2000.

Waddell-Rutter, Natalie. Personal letter (e-mail). January 25, 2001.

Walker, Stacy. Personal letter (e-mail). December 15, 2000.

Walsh, Danielle. Personal letter (e-mail). December 18, 2000.

Walters, John, "Bustin' Loose: Boxing took its act into virgin territory with a televised card from the Playboy Mansion," *Sports Illustrated* (May 29, 2000): 22.

Ward, Jessica. Personal letter (e-mail). January 5, 2000.

Wellman, Wendy. Personal letter (e-mail). January 15, 2001.

Wensel, Debz. Personal letters (e-mail). October 25, 2000 - January 1, 2001.

"Who We Are." Women's Sports and Fitness Foundation Malaysia website. Online: www.wsffm.org.

Wiechers, Brenda. Personal letter (e-mail). January 16, 2001.

Windhoek Conference. The International Working Group on Women and Sport website. Online: www.iwg-gti.org/e/windhoek/index.htm

Womack, Nancy. Personal letter (e-mail). December 12, 2000.

"Woman Placekicker's Lawsuit: Blue Devil of a Time," *Sports Illustrated* (October 23, 2000): 2.

"Women and Girls." The Sports Council for Wales website. Online: www.sports-council-wales.co.uk/whatsnew/women_girls.htm.

Women's Boxing Page website. Online: www.geocities.com/Colosseum/Field/6251.

Women's Sports Foundation Report. *Addressing the Needs of Female Professional and Amateur Athletes*. East Meadow, NY: Women's Sports Foundation, 1999.

Zimmerman, Jean and Gil Reavill. *Raising Our Athletic Daughters: How Sports Can Build Self- Esteem and Save Girls' Lives*. New York: Doubleday, 1998.

# INDEX